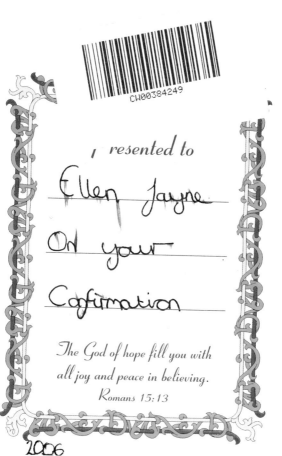

Presented to

Ellen Jayne

On your

Confirmation

The God of hope fill you with
all joy and peace in believing.
Romans 15:13

2006

CONFIRMATION
PRAYER BOOK

Stephen Lake is Sub Dean and Canon Residentiary of St Albans. Born in Dorset, he served his curacy at Sherborne Abbey before becoming vicar of Branksome St Aldhelm in Poole for more than nine years. He is married to Carol and they have three children.

CONFIRMATION PRAYER BOOK

Stephen Lake

Published in Great Britain in 2002 by
Society for Promoting Christian Knowledge
Holy Trinity Church
Marylebone Road
London NW1 4DU

British Library Cataloguing-in-Publication Data

A catalogue record for this book is available from the British Library

ISBN 0–281–05462–2 (white)
ISBN 0–281–05541–6 (blue)

3 5 7 9 10 8 6 4 2

Typeset by Pioneer Associates, Perthshire
Printed in Great Britain by
Bath Press-CPI, Bath

To
  Katie, Sam and Joe
    for your confirmation in faith

Contents

Foreword

This book should be in the hands of everyone who is being, or has been, confirmed. You will find encouragement to pray regularly and help in taking part in the Church's worship.

Stephen Lake is an experienced parish priest, who knows how to communicate his enthusiasm for the faith.

David Stancliffe
Bishop of Salisbury
Chair of the Liturgical Commission
of the Church of England

Introduction

This book is for you. It is your companion now that you have been confirmed. Whether you are an adult or a teenager you will find help here for your life as a Christian. Companions are great to make a journey with, but no matter how good your friend, you still have to make the effort to travel yourself. By being baptized and confirmed, you have made an important first step along the road to Christian maturity.

This book falls naturally into three main sections: 'Christian worship', 'Christian confidence', and 'Christian action'.

Christian worship
This first part will be useful for your daily life as a Christian. Use this as a way into prayer and worship.

Christian confidence
This second part is a helpful summary of some Christian teaching that you can return to for reference. It will help you to become more confident as a Christian.

Christian action
This third part encourages you to look outward and to fulfil your Christian potential in the world. There is resource material to help you put your faith into action.

Keep this book near you, along with your Bible. It will not last for ever, but if you do your best throughout your life as a confirmed person, your faith will indeed last for ever.

To start your journey from here as you mean to go on, read and reflect upon this wonderful story: Luke chapter 24.13–35: 'The Road to Emmaus'.

Christian worship

Prayer every day

Christians pray every day. That is how we live out our lives as Christians. Christians pray. God is always there to listen and to answer prayer, even if his answer is not always the one we might expect or hope for!

We cannot live as Christians if we do not pray, and praying is not just about going to church. Prayer is for every day and in every place. There are ways of shaping each day to help us to pray.

Morning prayers

There is no better way to start a day than with prayer. Many Christians get up especially early to greet the new day with prayer and praise, commending each day to God. However, mornings can be really busy as everybody goes off to work or school, all around the same time. In praying, you have to find what time of day works for you and do your best to stick with it. I'm a night owl myself, being able to carry on well into the early hours, but others may find prayer at the start of each day gets them going just as well as the latest breakfast cereal.

Here are some useful morning prayers. You can find an outline for a short morning prayer (or office) on p. 15.

As we rejoice in the gift of this new day,
so may the light of your presence, O God,
set our hearts on fire with love for you;
now and for ever. **Amen.**

Morning Prayer, *Common Worship*

3

This is the day that the Lord has made;
let us rejoice and be glad in it.

Psalm 118.24

O Lord, our heavenly Father,
almighty and everlasting God,
who hast safely brought us to the beginning of this day;
defend us in the same with thy mighty power;
and grant that this day we fall into no sin,
neither run into any kind of danger,
but that all our doings may be ordered by thy governance,
to do always that is righteous in thy sight;
through Jesus Christ our Lord.
Amen.

Morning Prayer, *Common Worship*

O Lord, enable us this day to reveal your glory in all we
think and say and do; that your presence may bless and
strengthen us all the day long, through Jesus Christ our
Lord. **Amen.**

Michael Saward

As well as prayers, Christians recite psalms and canticles from
the Bible at special times of day. The most popular and traditional morning canticle is the Benedictus or The Song of
Zechariah (Luke 1.68–79). Here, Zechariah, the father of John
the Baptist, rejoices at the naming of his son, and his voice,
which has been silent since he questioned the news of this
birth, is freed again to speak. This song is called the
Benedictus because of the Latin translation of the first word,
and this has traditionally been the biblical act of praise said in
the morning.

Blessed be the Lord the God of Israel,
who has come to his people and set them free.
He has raised up for us a mighty Saviour,
born of the house of his servant David.
Through his holy prophets God promised of old
to save us from our enemies,
     from the hands of all that hate us,
To show mercy to our ancestors,
and to remember his holy covenant.
This was the oath God swore to our father Abraham:
to set us free from the hands of our enemies,
Free to worship him without fear,
holy and righteous in his sight all the days of our life.
And you, child, shall be called the prophet of the Most
     High,
for you will go before the Lord to prepare his way,
To give his people knowledge of salvation
by the forgiveness of all their sins.
In the tender compassion of our God
the dawn from on high shall break upon us,
To shine on those who dwell in darkness and the
     shadow of death,
and to guide our feet into the way of peace.

Glory to the Father and to the Son
and to the Holy Spirit;
as it was in the beginning is now
and shall be for ever. **Amen.**

Common Worship (ELLC)

Midday prayers

Prayer during the day is often the best time for busy people. Even a one-hour lunch break can contain five minutes of prayer. It doesn't matter exactly what the time is but the chance to pray after some of the day has passed, and to pray about what is to come, can often enable the day to get off to a better second half.

Here are some useful prayers for during the day.

Lead us from death to life,
from falsehood to truth.
Lead us from despair to hope,
from fear to trust.
Lead us from hate to love,
from war to peace.
Let peace fill our hearts, our world, our universe.
Amen.

Satish Kumar

Pour your grace into our hearts, O Lord,
that as we have known the incarnation
of your Son Jesus Christ
by the message of an angel,
so by his cross and passion
we may be brought to the glory of his resurrection;
through Jesus Christ our Lord. **Amen.**

From the Collect for the Annunciation (the Angelus),
Common Worship

Evening prayers

There is an ancient Christian service that focuses on the lighting of the lamps as darkness approaches. This is called the Blessing of the Light or the Lucernarium. We take light for granted these days, being able to change our environment by the flick of a switch, but down the centuries people have seen the onset of darkness as a time of fear, threat and evil. Christians have always sought to brighten the darkness with the light that comes from Christ and so evening time is an especially good time to pray. You can light a candle of your own, or visit a cathedral which always has a service of sung evensong every day of the year, or use the time to reflect on the day now past.

There are lots of evening prayers.

Blessed are you, sovereign God,
our light and our salvation;
to you be glory and praise for ever.
You led your people to freedom
by a pillar of cloud by day and a pillar of fire by night.
May we who walk in the light of your presence
acclaim your Christ, rising victorious,
as he banishes all darkness from our hearts and minds.
Blessed be God, Father, Son and Holy Spirit:
Blessed be God for ever.

Evening Prayer, *Common Worship*

Lighten our darkness, we beseech thee, O Lord;
and by thy great mercy defend us
   from all perils and dangers of this night;
for the love of thy only Son, our Saviour, Jesus Christ.
Amen.

Evening Prayer, *Common Worship*

O Lord,
support us all the day long of this troublous life,
until the shadows lengthen, and the evening comes,
the busy world is hushed,
the fever of life is over
and our work is done.
Then, Lord, in your mercy grant us a safe lodging,
a holy rest, and peace at the last;
through Christ our Lord. **Amen.**

Common Worship: Pastoral Services

That this evening may be holy, good and peaceful:
We pray to you, O Lord.

That your holy angels may lead us
    in the paths of peace and goodwill:
We pray to you, O Lord.

That we may be pardoned and forgiven
    for our sins and offences:
We pray to you, O Lord.

That there may be peace in your Church
    and for the whole world:
We pray to you, O Lord.

That we may be bound together by your Holy Spirit
    in communion with all your saints,
    entrusting one another and all our life to Christ:
We pray to you, O Lord.

Society of Saint Francis

There is an evening Gospel canticle like the one for mornings.
It is the Song of Mary, the Magnificat from Luke 1.46–55.

Here the Blessed Virgin Mary responds to the message brought by the Archangel Gabriel that she is to bear a son. To 'magnify' is to declare the greatness of God, so the title comes again from the Latin translation of the first words, 'My soul magnifies . . .'. This canticle, along with the other Gospel canticles, is often set to music and sung by choirs and congregations. Another version can be found in the hymn by Bishop Timothy Dudley-Smith, 'Tell out, my soul'.

My soul proclaims the greatness of the Lord,
    my spirit rejoices in God my Saviour;
he has looked with favour on his lowly servant.
From this day all generations will call me blessed:
the Almighty has done great things for me
    and holy is his name.
He has mercy on those who fear him,
from generation to generation.
He has shown strength with his arm
and has scattered the proud in their conceit,
Casting down the mighty from their thrones
and lifting up the lowly.
He has filled the hungry with good things
and sent the rich away empty.
He has come to the aid of his servant Israel,
to remember his promise of mercy.
The promise made to our ancestors,
to Abraham and his children for ever.

Glory to the Father and to the Son
and to the Holy Spirit;
as it was in the beginning is now
and shall be for ever. **Amen.**

Common Worship (ELLC)

Tell out, my soul, the greatness of the Lord!
    Unnumbered blessings, give my spirit voice;
Tender to me the promise of his word;
    In God my Saviour shall my heart rejoice.

Tell out my soul, the greatness of his name!
    Make known his might, the deeds his arm has done;
His mercy sure, from age to age the same;
    His holy name, the Lord, the Mighty One.

Tell out, my soul, the greatness of his might!
    Powers and dominions lay their glory by.
Proud hearts and stubborn wills are put to flight,
    The hungry fed, the humble lifted high.

Tell out, my soul, the glories of his word!
    Firm is his promise, and his mercy sure.
Tell out, my soul, the greatness of the Lord
    To children's children and for evermore!

© Timothy Dudley-Smith

Night prayer

Night Prayer is also called Compline. This comes from the Latin word *completorium* meaning 'completion'. This is a time of quietness and reflection late at night before bed. It is a great way of ending a busy day, and if for some reason you have failed to pray during the day, here is your chance before the next day begins all over again.

Here are some suitable night prayers.

Before the ending of the day
Creator of the world, we pray
That you, with steadfast love, would keep
Your watch around us while we sleep.

From evil dreams defend our sight,
From fears and terrors of the night;
Tread underfoot our deadly foe
That we no sinful thought may know.

O Father, that we ask be done
Through Jesus Christ, your only Son;
And Holy Spirit, by whose breath
Our souls are raised to life from death.

Latin hymn

Save us, O Lord, while waking,
and guard us while sleeping,
that awake we may watch with Christ
and asleep may rest in peace.

Traditional

The Gospel canticle for Night Prayer is known as the Nunc Dimittis and is the Song of Simeon from Luke 2.29–32.

Now, Lord, you let your servant go in peace:
your word has been fulfilled.
My own eyes have seen the salvation
which you have prepared in the sight of every people;
A light to reveal you to the nations
and the glory of your people Israel.

Glory to the Father and to the Son
and to the Holy Spirit;
as it was in the beginning is now
and shall be for ever. **Amen.**

Common Worship (ELLC)

Making prayer a way of life

There are many opportunities in each day for prayer. There are even short, sharp arrow prayers which you can use when time is really pressing, such as 'Lord, help me through this day. Amen.' God always knows our needs and concerns before we tell him about them in prayer. Some churches have daily prayers during the week in church, or house groups you can visit to be able to pray with others. Look out for these times in weekly notice sheets.

Mealtimes: Christians have always wanted to thank God for food. If we believe in a creator God then we can thank him for all the goodness and work that has gone into our mealtimes. 'Saying grace', either in company or to ourselves, is a good way of making sure we never take God's gifts for granted.

Here are some useful graces.

For what we are about to receive may the Lord make us truly thankful. **Amen.**

O Lord, bless this food to our use and ourselves to your service, and keep us ever mindful of the needs of others. **Amen.**

In a world where so many are hungry we thank you for food.
In a world where so many are lonely we thank you for each other. **Amen.**

A Girl Guide Grace

Travelling: the whole Christian life is a journey into faith, so travelling has a special symbolism for Christians. Pilgrims travel over continents to visit places of prayer and hope, such as the Holy Land. Modern life is all about travelling; half an hour on the school bus, stuck in the monotonous traffic jam or standing on the familiar train – these are all opportunities for prayer that can otherwise be wasted in mindless nonsense. Travelling can also be a dangerous business, so prayer can be a natural stress-buster.

May our Lord Jesus Christ go before us to guide us;
stand behind us to give us strength;
and watch over us to protect us as we travel. **Amen.**

Prayer is an amazing thing. For the Christian it gives us personal access to God who gives us personal response. He is there to make it work for us – all we have to do is do it!

One way of doing prayer regularly is to say an 'office'. This means to set aside some time each day to pray according to a regular structure. All clergy are obliged to say their daily office in the form of morning and evening prayer. Here is a simple office that you may choose to use. It can be added to as you develop your regular praying pattern. As you grow into using this, ask your clergy how you can develop this prayer time further.

It can help to say the words of the office out loud or to mouth the words with your lips so that you don't rush this valuable time with God in prayer.

A simple prayer office

Spend a few moments collecting your thoughts, stilling yourself and focusing on God.

Introduction

O Lord, open our lips;
And our mouth shall proclaim your praise.

**Glory to the Father and to the Son
and to the Holy Spirit;
as it was in the beginning is now
and shall be for ever. Amen.**

The Liturgy of the Word

Now you may like to read a psalm. (Use one psalm each time you use this office.)

Now you may read from the Bible. (Why not begin by working through the passages on pp. 87–91?)

Pause for thought.

Now you may say a Gospel canticle, perhaps the Benedictus (p. 5) if it is morning, the Magnificat (p. 9) if it is evening, or the Nunc Dimittis (pp. 11–12) if it is night time.

Prayers

Here you can make prayer intentions, for the world, for people in need, for those you know and love, for the sick and the bereaved.

End with the Lord's Prayer.

Conclusion

Let us bless the Lord.
Thanks be to God.

Sharing in the Eucharist

Christians have a meal, given to us by Jesus himself, that is a sign of his presence with us. It has different names, all of which are good.

It is called Holy Communion, for we share communion with Christ himself; it is called the Eucharist, for it is a sharing of thanksgiving for all that God has done for us in Jesus; it is called the Lord's Supper, for as Jesus shared the last Passover meal with his disciples, so he shares his love with us; it is called the Mass (in Latin that is Missa) which connects it with our mission in the world.

Sharing

'The cup of blessing that we bless, is it not a sharing in the blood of Christ? The bread that we break, is it not a sharing in the body of Christ? Because there is one bread, we who are many are one body, for we all partake of the one bread' (1 Corinthians 10.16–17).

In receiving communion, we are also sharing our common purpose with other Christians; as we share Jesus we become more like him and as a church we can become more effective disciples. As the old saying goes, we celebrate 'the Lord's service on the Lord's day in the Lord's house'.

The *Common Worship* Holy Communion says:

> We break this bread
> To share in the body of Christ.
> *All* **Though we are many, we are one body,
> because we all share in one bread.**

Made one

We are made one by sharing Christ's brokenness. We are one because of Christ's death: in the words of *Common Worship*: 'Gather into one in your kingdom all who share this one bread and one cup' (Eucharistic Prayer B).

The sacrifice of Christ

We are caught up into the eternal self-offering of the Son to the Father. In the words of *Common Worship*: 'Father, we plead with confidence his sacrifice made once for all upon the cross' (Eucharistic Prayer G).

A foretaste of heaven

We share in the banquet of heaven. In the words of *Common Worship*: 'May we . . . be welcomed at your feast in heaven, where all creation worships you' (Eucharistic Prayer D).

Careful preparation

We should all receive holy communion as often as possible, especially on a Sunday, the day of the resurrection of Christ. We can receive communion every week, some even every day, but this still requires careful preparation.

Contrary to the way many diaries are laid out and to the way weekends feel, Sunday is traditionally the first day of the week. To think about Sunday in this way makes it a springboard for the coming seven days. You may like to prepare by looking at the set readings in the Lectionary, or by making a list of the people and concerns that you want to pray for. In receiving communion, you can then be ready to hear God's word, to pray and to be sent out into a new week, ready for action.

So careful devotional preparation before a communion service is important for every communicant. *Common Worship* provides 'A Form of Preparation' that can be used by an individual or a group before a Eucharist. It includes an 'Exhortation' and the 'Comfortable Words'.

Exhortation

As we gather at the Lord's table we must recall the promises and warnings given to us in the Scriptures and so examine ourselves and repent of our sins. We should give thanks to God for his redemption of the world through his Son Jesus Christ and, as we remember Christ's death for us and receive the pledge of his love, resolve to serve him in holiness and righteousness all the days of our life.

The Comfortable Words

Hear the words of comfort our Saviour Christ says to all who truly turn to him:

Come to me, all who labour and are heavy laden, and I will give you rest.   Matthew 11.28

God so loved the world that he gave his only-begotten Son,
that whoever believes in him should not perish but have eternal life.   John 3.16

Hear what Saint Paul says:
This saying is true, and worthy of full acceptance, that Christ Jesus came into the world to save sinners.
                    I Timothy 1.15

Hear what Saint John says:
If anyone sins, we have an advocate with the Father,
Jesus Christ the righteous;
and he is the propitiation for our sins.   1 John 2.1, 2

This traditional form can be used the evening before receiving communion:

In peace, we will lie down and sleep;
For you alone, Lord, make us dwell in safety.

Abide with us, Lord Jesus,
for the night is at hand and the day is now past.

As the night-watch looks for the morning,
so do we look for you, O Christ.

Come with the dawning of the day
**And make yourself known in the breaking of
    the bread.**

Night Prayer, *Common Worship*

Think now about when you are going to receive communion next and then set yourself some time to prepare for this wonderful gift.

Structure of the Eucharist

No two celebrations of the Eucharist are ever the same. The readings are different, the congregation is different each time, various prayers can change, and each priest will preside in a different way. There many options with prayers so that the different times of the year can be reflected and so that the cares and the concerns of the people can be valued.

There are four main types of communion service in the Church of England: Order One, Order One in Traditional Language, Order Two which follows the Book of Common Prayer tradition and Order Two in Contemporary Language. The most common of these is Order One, which is used throughout this book. Despite all the variations and possibilities, the Eucharist has a clear structure.

Order One

The people and the priest

- greet each other in the Lord's name

- confess their sins and are assured of God's forgiveness

- keep silence and pray a Collect

- proclaim and respond to the word of God

- pray for the Church and the world

- exchange the Peace

- prepare the table

- pray the Eucharistic Prayer

- break the bread

- receive communion

- depart with God's blessing

Step by step through the Eucharist

The Gathering

The people and priest . . .
. . . greet each other in the Lord's name

When friends come together they greet each other. We have always made a special point of the moment of greeting, which comes from the early days of our faith when Christians had to meet in secret and perhaps even exchange secret signs or passwords so as not be discovered. Now we know that we cannot worship together if we cannot greet each other, even if the greeting is a formal one to set the liturgy going.

This first part of the communion service is called the Gathering. The president may say an opening phrase commending the whole activity to God, Father, Son and Holy Spirit. The Greeting itself is a two-way acknowledgement using either:

> *The president greets the people*
>
> The Lord be with you
>
> All **and also with you.**
>
> (*or*)
>
> Grace, mercy and peace
> from God our Father
> and the Lord Jesus Christ
> be with you
>
> All **and also with you.**
>
> *From Easter Day to Pentecost this acclamation follows*
>
> Alleluia. Christ is risen.
>
> All **He is risen indeed. Alleluia.**

Words of welcome or introduction may then be said which often describe the theme for the day or point forwards to the message of the coming readings, especially the Gospel reading of the day.

Another prayer of preparation may be said called the Collect for Purity. This is a really good prayer to learn off by heart.

All **Almighty God,**
to whom all hearts are open,
all desires known,
and from whom no secrets are hidden:
cleanse the thoughts of our hearts
by the inspiration of your Holy Spirit,
that we may perfectly love you,
and worthily magnify your holy name;
through Christ our Lord.
Amen.

The people and the priest . . .
. . . confess their sins and are assured of God's forgiveness

Saying sorry is something we all have to do, and regularly too! We are rarely short of things to bring before God for his forgiveness. So it is important that we have this opportunity early on in the service so that we can receive communion faithfully. This section is called the Prayers of Penitence and may vary according to the season (different words can be used, for example, whether it is Christmas or Lent and so on). If you have made careful preparation before coming to receive communion you will be aware of your shortcomings and hopeful of the sign of God's love that the absolution can give. This is an opportunity for everyone together to examine their conscience both as individuals and as a community. The introduction to the words of confession sum up why we should take this seriously.

> God so loved the world
> that he gave his only Son Jesus Christ
> to save us from our sins,
> to be our advocate in heaven,
> and to bring us to eternal life.
>
> Let us confess our sins in penitence and faith,
> firmly resolved to keep God's commandments
> and to live in love and peace with all.

There are options for the words of confession but the most familiar is often learnt by heart.

> *All* **Almighty God, our heavenly Father,**
> **we have sinned against you**
> **and against our neighbour**
> **in thought and word and deed,**
> **through negligence, through weakness,**
> **through our own deliberate fault.**
> **We are truly sorry**
> **and repent of all our sins.**
> **For the sake of your Son Jesus Christ,**
> **who died for us,**
> **forgive us all that is past**
> **and grant that we may serve you in newness**
> **of life**
> **to the glory of your name.**
> **Amen.**

The words 'Lord, have mercy' and 'Christ, have mercy' may now be used, and may have specific intentions with them. They may also be sung, by the people or led by a choir. Traditionally, these words are called the Kyrie eleison, the Greek for 'Lord, have mercy'.

The words of the priest declare God's forgiveness and restore our relationship with God and with each other.

> Almighty God,
> who forgives all who truly repent,
> have mercy upon you,
> pardon and deliver you from all your sins,
> confirm and strengthen you in all goodness,
> and keep you in life eternal;
> through Jesus Christ our Lord.

All **Amen.**

The natural response to such a wonderful assurance is to praise God. Christians have a great song of praise called the Gloria in excelsis meaning 'Glory to God in the highest'. This can be said or is best sung while standing. The words bring to mind the song of the angels over the shepherds' fields at Jesus' birth. The Gloria is not usually used in Lent or Advent as they are penitential seasons.

All **Glory to God in the highest**
and peace to his people on earth.

Lord God, heavenly King,
almighty God and Father,
we worship you, we give you thanks,
we praise you for your glory.

Lord Jesus Christ, only Son of the Father,
Lord God, Lamb of God,
you take away the sin of the world:
have mercy on us;
you are seated at the right hand of the
    Father:
receive our prayer.

For you alone are the Holy One,
you alone are the Lord,
you alone are the Most High, Jesus Christ,
with the Holy Spirit,
in the glory of God the Father.
Amen.

The people and the priest . . .
. . . keep silence and pray a Collect

After a brief pause for silent reflection, the priest says a prayer that changes each week. This is called the Collect and is the special prayer, used by all the Church of England on that Sunday. This is a 'collecting prayer' that brings together the principles of the service and the prayers of the gathered community.

The Liturgy of the Word

The people and the priest . . .
. . . proclaim and respond to the word of God

Now the service has changed gear. After all the introductory material we now move into the Liturgy of the Word where we hear and respond to God's message. Usually, there are one or two readings before the Gospel reading. The readings are set for that particular day and come from what is called a lectionary. The first reading is usually from the Old

Testament. Then might follow a psalm, said or sung, and then a reading from the New Testament. Gradually the message of the day begins to unfold, culminating in the Gospel reading, which may be heralded by an Alleluia acclamation. We stand for the Gospel reading and make our response.

The Gospel is an important hinge-point of any Eucharist. We proclaim the good news of Jesus Christ by reading aloud his own words and actions as recorded by the Gospel writers and seek to apply this teaching to our lives today.

Next comes the sermon, which is usually a reflection on the readings and is an opportunity to expand on their meaning. Sermons should be meaningful and uplifting (not always so!) so our natural response is to the faith that has just been proclaimed to us. The way in which Christians of all traditions do this is in the words of a creed. This is a summary of the Christian faith agreed by all those who hold to our historic belief. You will have made a statement of faith at your confirmation.

The most commonly used creed is the Nicene Creed used on Sundays and Principal Holy Days. This was agreed by the Church, gathered together in Council at Nicaea as long ago as AD 325, as a statement by those about to be baptized. We usually stand for the saying of the creed.

All **We believe in one God,**
the Father, the Almighty,
maker of heaven and earth,
of all that is,
seen and unseen.

We believe in one Lord, Jesus Christ,
the only Son of God,

eternally begotten of the Father,
God from God, Light from Light,
true God from true God,
begotten, not made,
of one Being with the Father;
through him all things were made.
For us and for our salvation
    he came down from heaven,
was incarnate from the Holy Spirit
    and the Virgin Mary
and was made man.
For our sake he was crucified under
    Pontius Pilate;
he suffered death and was buried.
On the third day he rose again
in accordance with the Scriptures;
he ascended into heaven
and is seated at the right hand of the Father.
He will come again in glory
    to judge the living and the dead,
and his kingdom will have no end.

We believe in the Holy Spirit,
the Lord, the giver of life,
who proceeds from the Father and the Son,
who with the Father and the Son
    is worshipped and glorified,
who has spoken through the prophets.
We believe in one holy catholic and
    apostolic Church.
We acknowledge one baptism
    for the forgiveness of sins.

We look for the resurrection of the dead, and the life of the world to come. Amen.

The people and the priest . . .
. . . pray for the Church and the world

This is the time for the 'prayers of the people'. Obviously people have been praying up to this point, but the Prayers of Intercession enable the community to express their cares and concerns. A lay person, who may well have written the prayers personally, often leads the prayers. The task is to pray on behalf of the people, not to give another sermon telling God all he needs to know. There is a structure for these prayers:

We pray for:

- the Church of Christ;
- creation, human society, the Sovereign and those in authority;
- the local community;
- those who suffer;
- the communion of saints;
- those who have died.

Responses may be used between the intentions. If you have someone in particular need of prayer, say if they are sick, you can always ask before the service starts for their name to be included in the prayers. You may also find that the time will come when you will be asked by your church to share in the leading of intercessions. This is a privilege that carries a joyful responsibility.

The Liturgy of the Sacrament

The people and the priest . . .
. . . exchange the Peace

This part of the service is called the Liturgy of the Sacrament. Jesus said that we should be reconciled to our neighbour before bringing our gift to the altar so it is right that, having heard and participated in the Liturgy of the Word, we should exchange a sign of peace with each other before receiving Jesus in the next part. This is usually a handshake or something similar, depending on the familiarity of the people present. Some churches are more or less formal about this moment. The Peace is not just about the people sitting near you, whom you may not know; it is also a symbol of the peace that Christ offers to humankind.

The people and the priest . . .
. . . prepare the table

A hymn may be sung. During this, bread and wine are brought to the holy table or altar, as signs of God's gifts to us in creation. We offer to God gifts from all he has given us. We also offer ourselves, our souls and bodies. This is known as the 'offertory'.

The collection of money is often made at this point. Christians feel called to give because we have a giving Lord. We all have a part to play in the financial needs of the Church and the local community. The Bible encourages us to give sacrificially. Ask your church about the best way to give money to the Church. All of these signs and actions lead us on to the self-giving of Christ on the cross that the Eucharist celebrates.

The priest 'takes' the bread and wine. This is the first of four actions that recall the actions of Jesus at the Last Supper.

We 'take', we 'bless', we 'break', we 'share'. You will be able to see all of these actions in every Eucharist. Words may accompany all that is going on – here is an example.

> Blessed are you, Lord God of all creation:
> through your goodness we have this bread to set
>   before you,
> which earth has given and human hands have made.
> It will become for us the bread of life.

All **Blessed be God for ever.**

> Blessed are you, Lord God of all creation:
> through your goodness we have this wine to set
>   before you,
> fruit of the vine and work of human hands.
> It will become for us the cup of salvation.

All **Blessed be God for ever.**

The people and the priest ...
... pray the Eucharistic Prayer
This is the climax of the service. There are eight prayers and the priest will choose one; they are all different in character and style. The prayer may be accompanied by music and singing and ceremonial. There are a variety of congregational responses.

> Gathered around the altar table, with bread and wine as their focus, the president and people now pray the eucharistic prayer, a sustained outpouring of praise, that identifies with Jesus in the second of the four actions at the supper, but develops beyond this into thanksgiving

for the mighty acts of God in Christ himself, recalls the supper and the words during it, calls down the Holy Spirit in relation to the gifts and the people, and offers the duty and service of Christian hearts.

Michael Perham, *New Handbook of Pastoral Liturgy*

The aim is to make the prayer your own. Listen to the words telling the story of our salvation and open your heart to God in all his glory.

Immediately after the Eucharistic Prayer comes the Lord's Prayer. There are two different translations of this prayer.

As our Saviour taught us, so we pray

All **Our Father in heaven,**
hallowed be your name,
your kingdom come,
your will be done,
on earth as in heaven.
Give us today our daily bread.
Forgive us our sins
as we forgive those who sin against us.
Lead us not into temptation
but deliver us from evil.
For the kingdom, the power,
and the glory are yours
now and for ever.
Amen.

(or)

Let us pray with confidence as our Saviour has taught us

All **Our Father, who art in heaven,**
hallowed be thy name;
thy kingdom come;
thy will be done;
on earth as it is in heaven.
Give us this day our daily bread.
And forgive us our trespasses,
as we forgive those who trespass against us.
And lead us not into temptation;
but deliver us from evil.
For thine is the kingdom,
the power and the glory,
for ever and ever.
Amen.

The people and the priest . . .
. . . break the bread

This is the third of the actions of the Eucharist. The bread, whether it is communion wafer or loaf, is broken in order to be shared. But this is also about 'brokenness'. As Christ's body was broken for us on the cross so our own brokenness and the brokenness of the Church is symbolically represented in this action.

We break this bread
to share in the body of Christ.

All **Though we are many, we are one body,**
because we all share in one bread.

(or)

Every time we eat this bread
and drink this cup,

All **we proclaim the Lord's death**
until he comes.

The Agnus Dei may follow here and is often sung, sometimes as the bread continues to be broken. The words make the connection between what is going on and the broken body on the cross.

All   **Lamb of God,**
you take away the sin of the world,
have mercy on us.

Lamb of God,
you take away the sin of the world,
have mercy on us.

Lamb of God,
you take away the sin of the world,
grant us peace.

(or)

All   **Jesus, Lamb of God,**
have mercy on us.

Jesus, bearer of our sins,
have mercy on us.

Jesus, redeemer of the world,
grant us peace.

The people and the priest ...
... receive communion
The president now invites the people to communion. This is another one of those prayers that it is good to learn off by heart as part of our own treasury of prayers.

Jesus is the Lamb of God
who takes away the sin of the world.
Blessed are those who are called to his supper.

All **Lord, I am not worthy to receive you,
but only say the word, and I shall be healed.**

The Prayer of Humble Access sometimes follows now. It is a traditional prayer for humility before receiving this wonderful sacrament.

All **We do not presume
to come to this your table, merciful Lord,
trusting in our own righteousness,
but in your manifold and great mercies.
We are not worthy
so much as to gather up the crumbs under
your table.
But you are the same Lord
whose nature is always to have mercy.
Grant us therefore, gracious Lord,
so to eat the flesh of your dear Son
Jesus Christ
and to drink his blood,
that our sinful bodies may be made clean
by his body
and our souls washed
through his most precious blood,
and that we may evermore dwell in him,
and he in us.
Amen.**

Everyone receives communion in the form of consecrated bread and wine. Most usually, this means receiving kneeling or standing.

Some may need to receive a gluten-free wafer and some may choose to receive bread or wine only. Some may choose to 'intinct' their wafer by dipping it in the chalice of wine. Some may need the sacrament brought to them because of their infirmity. All methods are authentic methods of receiving communion.

Children who have been admitted to communion will also receive.

Some of the sacrament may be reserved for the communion of the sick on another occasion.

After communion it is best to spend a moment in quiet reflection. There will be prayers of thanksgiving after everyone has received. Two of the most popular are as follows.

All **Almighty God,**
we thank you for feeding us
with the body and blood of your Son
Jesus Christ.
Through him we offer you our souls
and bodies
to be a living sacrifice.
Send us out
in the power of your Spirit
to live and work
to your praise and glory.
Amen.

(or)

All **Father of all,**
we give you thanks and praise,
that when we were still far off
you met us in your Son and brought us home.
Dying and living, he declared your love,
gave us grace, and opened the gate of glory.
May we who share Christ's body live his
risen life;
we who drink his cup bring life to others;
we whom the Spirit lights give light to
the world.
Keep us firm in the hope you have set
before us,
so we and all your children shall be free,
and the whole earth live to praise your name;
through Christ our Lord.
Amen.

The Dismissal

The people and the priest . . .
. . . depart with God's blessing

Being 'sent out' is very much an integral part of the service. Again, actions speak as loud as words, for, having received Christ, we are sent out to proclaim him and do his work in the world. The dismissal contains a blessing by the priest and words, perhaps spoken by a deacon, to send you out with a heart for mission. As you leave church, just imagine all the people all over the world being sent out from a Eucharist, energized to share the Good News of Jesus Christ. You have your part in God's plan.

Go in peace to love and serve the Lord.

All **In the name of Christ. Amen.**

Day by day through the year

There is a wonderful prayer based on one by St Richard of Chichester that helps us pray that we might draw ever closer to God – day by day.

> Thanks be to you, our Lord Jesus Christ,
> for all the benefits you have given us,
> for all the pains and insults you have borne for us.
> O merciful redeemer, friend and brother,
> may we know you more clearly,
> love you more dearly,
> and follow you more nearly,
> day by day. **Amen.**

Every day is special to God. Every day is new and full of potential. As Christians, we believe that it is the privilege of the Church to celebrate the passage of time as a gift that God has given us and as a responsibility for us to use to his glory.

You will have your special days that you like to celebrate. Some days are easy to remember, like your birthday: others are more difficult to remember, like someone else's birthday or a wedding anniversary. We keep diaries and calendars and write ourselves reminders.

My birthday: _____

My baptism date: _____

My confirmation date: _____

Other dates to remember: _____

_____

_____

_____

The Christian Year

The Church has a way of telling and re-telling the mighty acts of God, and of celebrating his continuing presence and activity in the world. It is called the Calendar, which in turn is supported by a lectionary.

Calendar: the celebration of time and seasons
Lectionary: the list of agreed Bible readings for each and every day

The most familiar Sunday Lectionary in use in the Church of England is used by many other denominations and follows a three-year cycle. Each day is provided with specially chosen readings and Sundays and other Principal Holy Days and Saints' Days are given particular readings (or lections). Each of the three years concentrates on one of the Gospels: Year A Matthew; Year B Mark; Year C Luke; with John's Gospel being read on particular days across the three years. You can buy small copies of the lists of readings in the Lectionary or you can buy a book which prints out all the readings, such as the *Revised Common Lectionary* (Mowbray) or the *Common Worship Lectionary* (OUP).

ALL SAINTS (Gold)

ORDINARY (Green)

CHRIST THE KING (Gold)

ADVENT (Purple)

CHRISTMAS (Gold)

EPIPHANY (white)

CANDLEMAS

L (Purple)

TIME
Sundays after Trinity

TRINITY
(Gold)

dm

PENTECOST
(Red)

ASCENSION

EASTER

EASTER (Gold)
GOOD FRIDAY
MAUNDY THURSDAY
PALM SUNDAY

T

Sundays

All Sundays are special days as they celebrate the Easter story of the death and resurrection of the Lord. While each Sunday will be different in character, they are all celebrations of the first Easter Day.

The seasons

On pages 40–41 there is a simplified outline of the year. Some days may vary according to the particular date of Easter each year. The picture shows the Church's year in a circle, and you start on the left with Advent, move through Christmas and so on until you return at the end of the circle. The colours named in this picture are the liturgical colours used in church that day.

Advent

The First Sunday of Advent
The Second Sunday of Advent
The Third Sunday of Advent
The Fourth Sunday of Advent
Christmas Eve

Christmas Day – *25 December*

The First Sunday of Christmas
The Second Sunday of Christmas

Epiphany – *6 January*

The Baptism of Christ, The First Sunday of Epiphany
The Second Sunday of Epiphany
The Third Sunday of Epiphany

The Fourth Sunday of Epiphany
**The Presentation of Christ in the Temple
(Candlemas)** – *2 February*

Ordinary Time

The Fifth Sunday before Lent
The Fourth Sunday before Lent
The Third Sunday before Lent
The Second Sunday before Lent
The Sunday next before Lent

Lent

Ash Wednesday
The First Sunday of Lent
The Second Sunday of Lent
The Third Sunday of Lent
The Fourth Sunday of Lent –
    Mothering Sunday
The Fifth Sunday of Lent
Palm Sunday
Monday, Tuesday, Wednesday of
    Holy Week
Maundy Thursday
Good Friday
Easter Eve

Easter Day

Monday to Saturday of Easter Week
The Second Sunday of Easter
The Third Sunday of Easter

The Fourth Sunday of Easter
The Fifth Sunday of Easter
The Sixth Sunday of Easter
Ascension Day
The Seventh Sunday of Easter
Pentecost (Whit Sunday)

Ordinary Time

Trinity Sunday
The Day of Thanksgiving for the Institution of
     Holy Communion (Corpus Christi) –
     Thursday after Trinity Sunday
The First Sunday after Trinity
Up to another twenty-one Sundays after Trinity
Dedication Festival
All Saints' Day – *1 November*
The Fourth Sunday before Advent
The Third Sunday before Advent
The Second Sunday before Advent
Christ the King – *The Sunday next before Advent*

 Principal feasts
    These are the most important days of the year
alongside ordinary Sundays. On these days the Holy Communion is celebrated in every cathedral and parish church.

Christmas Day
The Baptism of Christ (Epiphany 1 usually)
The Epiphany

The Presentation of Christ in the Temple
The Annunciation of Our Lord to the Blessed Virgin Mary
Easter Day
Ascension Day
Pentecost (Whit Sunday)
Trinity Sunday
All Saints' Day

There are some other Principal Holy Days that are part of Lent.

Ash Wednesday
Maundy Thursday
Good Friday

Some of these days have set dates, others will have their date moved according to the date of Easter. When you buy a diary at the beginning of the year, look for one that has the important Christian days included.

Festivals

These are special days that often have a service to mark that day.

The Naming and Circumcision of Jesus	*(1 January)*
The Conversion of Paul	*(25 January)*
Joseph of Nazareth	*(19 March)*
George, Martyr, Patron of England	*(23 April)*
Mark the Evangelist	*(25 April)*
Philip and James, Apostles	*(1 May)*

Matthias the Apostle	*(14 May)*
The Visit of the Blessed Virgin Mary to Elizabeth	*(31 May)*
Barnabas the Apostle	*(11 June)*
The Birth of John the Baptist	*(24 June)*
Peter and Paul, Apostles	*(29 June)*
Thomas the Apostle	*(3 July)*
Mary Magdalene	*(22 July)*
James the Apostle	*(25 July)*
The Transfiguration of Our Lord	*(6 August)*
The Blessed Virgin Mary	*(15 August)*
Bartholomew the Apostle	*(24 August)*
Holy Cross Day	*(14 September)*
Matthew, Apostle and Evangelist	*(21 September)*
Michael and All Angels	*(29 September)*
Luke the Evangelist	*(18 October)*
Simon and Jude, Apostles	*(28 October)*
Christ the King	*(Sunday next before Advent)*
Andrew the Apostle	*(30 November)*
Stephen, Deacon, First Martyr	*(26 December)*
John, Apostle and Evangelist	*(27 December)*
The Holy Innocents	*(28 December)*

Other special days

There are other days which may have importance because of a particular person or place. The Dedication Festival of a church is the anniversary of the date of its dedication or consecration. Harvest Thanksgiving can be celebrated on a suitable Sunday.

All Souls' Day (2 November) is a commemoration of all the faithful departed.

Liturgical colours

We use every gift of God to help us describe his amazing wonder and complexity. Just as readings change to mark a day, so the special clothes worn in church and the hangings change colour according to the season or feast day. Look out for the colour of the vestments worn by the clergy, the colour of an altar front and even hints in floral decorations. The colours have no meaning in themselves, but colour, light, darkness, music, dance all help us to articulate our praise for God's creation.

White or gold is the colour for festal periods like Christmas and Easter. It is the colour for Trinity Sunday, Festivals of our Lord and the Blessed Virgin Mary, All Saints' Day, saints other than martyrs, Baptism, Marriage and the funerals of children.

Red is used during Holy Week (except at Holy Communion on Maundy Thursday), on the Feast of Pentecost and may be used between All Saints' Day and Advent. It is appropriate for services which focus on the gift of the Holy Spirit and for saints remembered as martyrs.

Purple is the colour for Advent and Lent. It is often used for funerals (though black may also be used).

Green is used for Ordinary Time.

There may be local variations to these colours.

Saints in glory

It is often said that the best place to see a saint is in a stained-glass window. Full of colour and beauty, these figures look down on us as examples of Christian devotion. But they are not there because of their holiness and great deeds but because, like the window, the Light of Christ has shone through them to bring others to faith and to give us hope. The Church remembers the saints usually on the day that they died. There are of course many other saintly people from the past and indeed the present (you may know some-one that you think is a saint), but there are certain people through time that the Church chooses to remember.

Here are just a few of my favourites, one from each month.

Antony of Egypt, Hermit, Abbot   *17 January   White*

Born in 251, Antony heard the gospel message, 'If you would be perfect, go, sell your possessions, and give the money to the poor, and you will have treasure in heaven; then come, follow me.' He was twenty years old and rich, so gave up everything and went to live in the desert. He became a spiritual guide for many who flocked to him. He died in the year 356, asking that he be buried secretly, so that his person might be hidden in death as in life.

I like him because of his devotion and because he reminds me to spend time in prayer and to 'get away from it all' sometimes.

Valentine, Martyr at Rome, c. 269   *14 February   Red*

Valentine was a priest who was martyred at Rome under the Emperor Claudius. Few of us think of a real person when we think of Valentine's Day. For Christians, the day marks an acknowledgement of an all-loving God who blesses those who love one another, as Jesus implored his own disciples to do.

Oscar Romero, Archbishop of San Salvador

24 March Red

Not all saintly people are from long ago. Oscar Romero spoke out against violence in San Salvador and preached about the needs of the poor. He refused to be silenced and was gunned down while celebrating the Eucharist on this day in 1980. He means a great deal to me as a priest, because he reminds me never to take for granted the wonderful privilege of presiding at worship.

George, Patron Saint of England

23 April Red

St George was probably a soldier living in Palestine at the beginning of the fourth century. Tradition says that he killed a dragon, perhaps in truth a crocodile, and by saving the local community from this beast, he converted them to Christianity. Little is known about him that is accurate, but I like him because he is the patron saint of scouting with which I have always been involved.

Aldhelm, Bishop of Sherborne

25 May White

Born in 639, Aldhelm rose through the monastery at Malmesbury to become Bishop of the growing Wessex diocese. He was famed for his preaching, scholarship and music-making. One story tells of how he followed out of a church service those who left when the sermon began and, getting ahead of them, attracted them by his singing only to start preaching at them when they could no longer get away! I like him because I come from the same area and because my first parish was named St Aldhelm in Branksome, Dorset.

Alban, First Martyr of Britain 22 June Red

Alban was a soldier in the Roman city of Verulamium (now St Albans in Hertfordshire). He gave shelter to a Christian priest fleeing from persecution, hiding him in his house for several days. Alban received instruction from the priest and was converted. When the priest's hiding-place was discovered, Alban dressed himself in the priest's cloak and was arrested in his place. He was tortured and beheaded, probably in the year 250. He is special to me because, currently, I work at St Alban's Cathedral which stands on the site of his death.

Anne and Joachim 26 July White

First mentioned in the second century, they were the parents of the Blessed Virgin Mary. They remind us of God's plan from the beginning to send his Son, Jesus. I like to pray for my grandparents on this day.

The Blessed Virgin Mary 15 August White or gold

Mary was a young Jewish girl living in Nazareth when a messenger from the Lord announced that she was to be the bearer of the Son of God to the world. Her response 'Let it be to me according to your word' revealed her natural sense of obedience to God and her reverence for his word, showing her worthy to be the bearer of the Word made flesh. This day is now celebrated as the major feast of the Blessed Virgin Mary throughout most of Christendom.

Holy Cross Day   *14 September   Red*

The cross has become the universal symbol for Christianity, replacing the fish symbol of the early Church, though you can see the latter more frequently again these days. Early in the fourth century, Helena, the mother of the emperor, was said to have uncovered in Jerusalem a cross, believed to be the cross of Christ. A great basilica was built on the site of the Holy Sepulchre and dedicated on this day in the year 335. This day reminds me of visits to the Holy Land and so I pray for Christian unity.

Francis of Assisi   *4 October   White*

Francis is one of the most well-known saints. After leaving his rich upbringing, he was praying in the derelict church of St Damian when he distinctly heard the words 'Go and repair my church, which you see is falling down.' He founded the Franciscan Order.

Two years before his death, he received the stigmata, the marks of the wounds of Christ, on his body.

Catherine of Alexandria   *25 November   Red*

Tradition has it that Catherine was a fourth-century girl of a noble family who, because of her Christian faith, refused marriage with the emperor. She is said to have disputed with fifty philosophers whose job it was to convince her of her error and to have confounded them all. She was tortured by being splayed on a wheel (that's where firework Catherine wheels come from) and finally beheaded. This day is special in our family because Catherine is the patron saint to our daughter.

Nicholas, Bishop of Myra c. 326   *6 December*   *White*

This is the real Father Christmas! Nicholas loved children, healed the sick, fed the hungry and cared for the oppressed. He saved three girls by giving them dowries and was known for his good works all over southern Turkey. (The link between Christmas and Turkey is entirely coincidental.)

Who is your favourite saint?

_____

_____

_____

Who is your patron saint?

_____

_____

_____

It may not be instantly obvious who your patron saint is. You can use your first name or other Christian names that you have. For example, Tracy is derived from Teresa, hence St Theresa would be Tracy's patron saint. Likewise Dean is derived from Dennis, hence St Denys is Dean's patron saint. If there is more than one named saint you can choose the one whose story most fits you. So with my children, Katie's patron saint is St Catherine or Katharine of Alexandria (25 November), Samuel James's patron saint is St James the Apostle (25 July) and Joseph's patron saint is St Joseph of

Nazareth (19 March). There are many books about the saints, from which you can find out more.

The passage of time for Christians is a holy thing. We share in creation and celebrate it by our annual recalling of God's activity in the world. By living the Christian year, we praise God who is yesterday, today, for ever.

Seven signs

'Actions speak louder than words', or so it is said. There are a lot of words in our faith – readings, sermons, hymns – but we also need signs to help us be aware of God's presence and his activity in our lives. In the Church these are called the sacraments.

A sacrament is an outward and visible sign of an inward and spiritual gift (or grace) – in other words, something we can see or feel or experience, that has deep meaning, real impact, a changing influence, from God.

God knows that as human beings, we need such signs to help us along our journey. A handshake can mean much more than words of welcome, a kiss more than a spoken phrase, a personal apology face to face much more than a written note. God created us so that we can engage with him through material things and through aspects of nature. Simply, God takes simple, ordinary, everyday things and makes them holy for our use. Our prayer is that he does the same with us for his use.

There are seven sacraments. The first two are called dominical sacraments – instituted by Jesus himself – and five are called sacraments of the Church. They are:

- Holy Baptism
- the Eucharist
- Confirmation
- Absolution

- Marriage
- Ordination
- Holy Unction

Holy Baptism

Do you remember your baptism? If you were baptized (or christened) as a baby you probably won't remember the great day. If you were baptized when you were confirmed you most certainly will remember. Whether you were baptized as a babe in arms or as an adult you will have become a full member of the Christian Church and incorporated into the life, death and resurrection of Jesus Christ.

While Baptism is seen as the beginning of your Christian journey, it is also much more than that. Although the celebration of baptism is a once-only dying and rising, working out the consequences takes a lifetime. We become members of the Christian community so that we can partake in the life of God and share in the mission of God to the world.

The outward signs of baptism are pouring water over the candidate, anointing with oil, signing with the cross and the giving of a lighted candle. The inward and spiritual gifts are membership of the Church and incorporation into Jesus. In church, the furniture used for baptism is the font.

Here are two prayers from the Baptism service that help us understand its meaning:

Our Lord Jesus Christ has told us
that to enter the kingdom of heaven
we must be born again of water and the Spirit,
and has given us baptism as the sign and seal of this
    new birth.

Here we are washed by the Holy Spirit and made clean.
Here we are clothed with Christ,
dying to sin that we may live his risen life.
As children of God, we have a new dignity
and God calls us to fullness of life.

N and N,
today God has touched you with his love
and given you a place among his people.
God promises to be with you
in joy and in sorrow,
to be your guide in life,
and to bring you safely to heaven.
In baptism God invites you on a life-long journey.
Together with all God's people
you must explore the way of Jesus
and grow in friendship with God,
in love for his people,
and in serving others.
With us you will listen to the word of God
and receive the gifts of God.

The Eucharist

You may have been receiving communion since you were a child or, most likely, you have now started receiving communion since your confirmation. If Holy Baptism is the beginning of our faith, to be deepened through time, then Holy Communion is the food to sustain the baptized on the way. With communion it is important to receive regularly and faithfully.

The outward and visible signs of Holy Communion are

bread and wine, the inward and spiritual gift is the body and blood of Jesus. In church, we use for Holy Communion a holy table or altar.

Here is a prayer from the Eucharist that helps us prepare to receive communion:

All **Most merciful Lord,**
your love compels us to come in.
Our hands were unclean,
our hearts were unprepared:
we were not fit
even to eat the crumbs from under your
table.
But you, Lord, are the God of our salvation,
and share your bread with sinners.
So cleanse and feed us
with the precious body and blood of your Son,
that he may live in us and we in him;
and that we, with the whole company
of Christ,
may sit and eat in your kingdom.
Amen.

Confirmation

At your confirmation you will have 'confirmed' your Baptism and God will have 'confirmed' the activity of the Holy Spirit in you. The bishop said to you, '*N*, God has called you by name and made you his own.' The words are full of meaning as they remind us that all this is the activity of God who has been there in our lives from the beginning, calling us by name to do his will. In confirmation, as the bishop prays and lays on hands, the power of the Holy Spirit is given so that you may continue to grow in Christian strength and witness. Confirmation is in some ways, a 'coming of age', whatever age you may be.

The outward and visible signs of confirmation are the laying on of hands and anointing, the inward and spiritual gift is the power of the Holy Spirit. A bishop is the minister of confirmation.

Here is one of the prayers from the Confirmation service:

Almighty and ever-living God,
you have given these your servants new birth
in baptism by water and the Spirit,
and have forgiven them all their sins.
Let your Holy Spirit rest upon them:
the Spirit of wisdom and understanding;
the Spirit of counsel and inward strength;
the Spirit of knowledge and true godliness;
and let their delight be in the fear of the Lord. **Amen.**

Absolution

All people do or say things that are wrong. We all do or say things that can hurt others. You and I do or say things that are painful to God. As Christians, we should be aware of our shortcomings, set against the wonderful glory of God and his boundless love. Absolution is the assurance of God's forgiveness.

There are different ways in which we can examine our conscience and confess. First, we can join in the general confession in many of our services, being sure to make that confession our own. Second, we can make our confession to

God himself through personal prayer, through spending time with God and meditating on the ways in which we may have offended him.

Third, in order to be assured of the power of God's forgiveness, we may confess to a priest, who can offer counsel, suggestions for amendment of life and personal absolution, or we may talk to another wise person. The general rule with the sacrament of confession is that 'none must, all may, some should'. Your parish clergy will be able to advise you about how to grow into this sacrament if you would value help and reassurance over any matter that bothers you.

The outward and visible sign of absolution is the sign of the cross; the inward and spiritual gift is the forgiveness of sins.

Examining your conscience is not a popular exercise. Done well, it helps us to recognize not only our personal shortcomings but also the failure of humankind. We all have a part, even if it is merely indifference, in the sin of the world, where there is so much of the world short of food and water or peace and freedom. A meditation to help with a serious examination of conscience follows.

Here is a short act of penitence:

Spend some time in private prayer and perhaps read from the Bible (try Luke 15.11–32 or Luke 17.1–4).

Think about your sins and pray:

Almighty God,
long-suffering and of great goodness:
I confess to you,
I confess with my whole heart
my neglect and forgetfulness of your commandments,
my wrong doing, thinking, and speaking;

the hurts I have done to others,
and the good I have left undone.
O God, forgive me, for I have sinned against you;
and raise me to newness of life;
through Jesus Christ our Lord. **Amen.**

Pause for silent reflection then read:

God, the Father of mercies,
has reconciled the world to himself
through the death and resurrection of his Son,
    Jesus Christ,
not counting our trespasses against us,
but sending his Holy Spirit
to shed abroad his love among us.
By the ministry of reconciliation
entrusted by Christ to his Church,
receive his pardon and peace
to stand before him in his strength alone,
this day and evermore. **Amen.**

Pray a prayer of thanksgiving in your own words.

Marriage

The first miracle by Jesus as recorded in St John's Gospel was at a wedding. A wedding is one of life's great moments, a time of solemn commitment as well as good wishes, feasting and joy. We all have memories of happy wedding days.

For Christians, marriage is the foundation of family life and speaks to us of lifelong commitment that finds its theological root in the relationship of the Trinity. Obviously, though, families come in all shapes and sizes today and God's love is shared with all who follow him.

Common Worship makes this description of marriage.

Marriage is intended by God to be a creative relationship, as his blessing enables husband and wife to love and support each other in good times and in bad, and to share in the care and upbringing of children. For Christians, marriage is also an invitation to share life together in the spirit of Jesus Christ. It is based upon a solemn, public and life-long covenant between a man and a woman, declared and celebrated in the presence of God and before witnesses.

The outward and visible signs of marriage are the joining of hands, the making of solemn vows and the exchange of rings; the inward and spiritual gift is the joining of souls.

You may already be married or not, but knowing the Anglican marriage vow helps guide us in all our friendships and relationships.

I, *N*, take you, *N*,
to be my *wife/husband*,
to have and to hold
from this day forward;
for better, for worse,
for richer, for poorer,
in sickness and in health,
to love and to cherish,
till death us do part;
according to God's holy law.
In the presence of God I make this vow.

Ordination

I am ordained. I was ordained (or made) a deacon and then a year later ordained a priest. This means that I have been set apart for a particular form of ministry. Everyone who is baptized is called to ministry, often called 'every member ministry'. As you go about your daily life you will be ministering to others, and many people have powerful and valuable ministries that they exercise in the name of the Church.

Some people are called to be ordained. The orders of ordained ministry are: bishop (called to be a shepherd of God's people), priest (called to be a servant with specific tasks), deacon (called to be a servant).

The outward and visible sign of ordination is the laying on of hands and anointing, the inward and spiritual gift is the setting apart for service. Only a bishop can ordain.

Here is the Collect for the Fifth Sunday after Trinity:

Almighty and everlasting God,
by whose Spirit the whole body of the Church
   is governed and sanctified:
hear our prayer which we offer for all your faithful
   people,
that in their vocation and ministry
they may serve you in holiness and truth
to the glory of your name;
through our Lord and Saviour Jesus Christ,
who is alive and reigns with you,
in the unity of the Holy Spirit,
one God, now and for ever. **Amen.**

Holy Unction

This unfamiliar name describes the ministry of healing and wholeness that is offered by the Church. We are in the business of healing and wholeness, just as Jesus exercised this powerful ministry. At different times in our lives, especially when we are sick, we need prayer or communion or anointing with oil or the laying on of hands or all of these signs at once in order to feel safe in the hands of our heavenly Father. You will not see this ministry very often in church life, but it is the bread and butter of pastoral ministry as we share God's love with those in need.

The outward and visible signs of holy unction are the laying on of hands with anointing; the inward and spiritual gift is spiritual healing and wholeness.

This text can be used as an introduction to a time of prayer for wholeness and healing.

> Christ taught his disciples to love one another. In his community of love, in praying together, in sharing all things and in caring for the sick, they recalled his words: 'In so far as you did this to one of these, you did it to me.' We gather today to witness to this teaching and to pray in the name of Jesus the healer that the sick may be restored to health and that all among us may know his saving power.

You may well experience most or even all of the sacraments in your lifetime. They are there to touch your heart and in this way God's love reaches out to us, transforming ordinary things into wonderful gifts.

At all times and in all places

Christians pray everywhere and at any time. If prayer is our communication with God, then we will have many and varied opportunities and needs. Here are a series of resources to help you in the future.

 Traditional prayers

The Grace
The grace of our Lord Jesus Christ,
the love of God,
and the fellowship of the Holy Spirit
be with us evermore. **Amen.**

A morning collect
Almighty and everlasting God,
we thank you that you have brought us safely
to the beginning of this day.
Keep us from falling into sin
or running into danger,
order us in all our doings
and guide us to do always
what is righteous in your sight;
through Jesus Christ our Lord. **Amen.**

An evening collect

Lighten our darkness,
Lord, we pray,
and in your great mercy
defend us from all perils and dangers of this night,
for the love of your only Son,
our Saviour Jesus Christ. **Amen.**

A prayer of dedication

Almighty God,
we thank you for the gift of your holy word.
May it be a lantern to our feet,
a light to our paths,
and a strength to our lives.
Take us and use us
to love and serve
in the power of the Holy Spirit
and in the name of your Son,
Jesus Christ our Lord. **Amen.**

For the guidance of the Holy Spirit

God, who from of old
taught the hearts of your faithful people
by sending to them the light of your Holy Spirit:
grant us by the same Spirit
to have a right judgement in all things
and evermore to rejoice in his holy comfort;
through the merits of Christ Jesus our Saviour. **Amen.**

Summary of the Law

Our Lord Jesus Christ said:
The first commandment is this:
'Hear, O Israel, the Lord our God is the only Lord.
You shall love the Lord your God with all your heart,
with all your soul, with all your mind,
and with all your strength.'

The second is this: 'Love your neighbour as yourself.'
There is no other commandment greater than these.
On these two commandments hang all the law and
the prophets.

Amen. Lord, have mercy.

The Beatitudes

Let us hear our Lord's blessing on those who follow him.

Blessed are the poor in spirit,
for theirs is the kingdom of heaven.

Blessed are those who mourn,
for they shall be comforted.

Blessed are the meek,
for they shall inherit the earth.

Blessed are those who hunger and thirst after
righteousness,
for they shall be satisfied.

Blessed are the merciful,
for they shall obtain mercy.

Blessed are the pure in heart,
for they shall see God.

Blessed are the peacemakers,
for they shall be called children of God.

Blessed are those who suffer persecution for
righteousness' sake,
for theirs is the kingdom of heaven.

 Prayers of reassurance

St Patrick's Breastplate

Christ be with me, Christ within me,
Christ behind me, Christ before me,
Christ beside me, Christ to own me,
Christ to comfort and restore me.
Christ beneath me, Christ above me,
Christ in quiet, Christ in danger.
Christ in hearts of all who love me,
Christ in mouth of friend and stranger.

God be in my head

God be in my head,
and in my understanding;
God be in my eyes,
and in my looking;
God be in my mouth,
and in my speaking;
God be in my heart,
and in my thinking;
God be at my end,
and at my departing. **Amen.**

A Latin hymn of 1514

Prayer of St Francis of Assisi

Lord, make me an instrument of your peace:
where there is hatred let me sow peace,
where there is injury let me sow pardon,
where there is doubt let me sow faith,
where there is despair let me give hope,
where there is darkness let me give light,
where there is sadness let me give joy.
O Divine Master, grant that I may
not try to be comforted but to comfort,
not try to be understood but to understand,
not try to be loved but to love.
Because it is in giving that we receive,
it is in forgiving that we are forgiven,
and it is in dying that we are born to eternal life.

 ## Prayer at home

Visit this house, O Lord, we pray,
drive far from it all snares of the enemy;
may your holy angels dwell with us
and guard us in peace
and may your blessing always be upon us;
through Jesus Christ our Lord. **Amen.**

Common Worship: Pastoral Services

Blessed are you, Lord God,
king of all creation:
through your goodness you have given this house
     to be our home.
Let your peace remain with us always.

Let all who come here to share our life
find generosity, tranquillity and happiness;
may they depart enriched by the joy of Christian living.

Adapted from Pocket Ritual

 Prayers for all

In time of crisis

God of all care and compassion
you take us through deep waters
but never abandon us in the storm;
we walk in the dark
but you never leave us without light.
Be with us in the night of our anxiety
and in the day of our over-confidence
that we may keep faith with each other
as you have kept faith with us in
Jesus Christ our Lord. **Amen.**

Stephen Oliver

For the confirmed

God, our Father,
complete the work you have begun
and keep the gifts of your Holy Spirit active
in the hearts of those who have been confirmed.
Make them ready to live his gospel
and eager to do his will.
May they never be ashamed to proclaim
to all the world Christ crucified,
living and reigning for ever and ever. **Amen.**

Michael Buckley

A prayer for someone who has died

Listen to our prayers, Lord, as we humbly beg your mercy that the soul of your servant (*name*) whom you have called from this life may be brought by you to a place of peace and light; and so be enabled to share the life of all the saints, through Jesus Christ our Lord. **Amen.**

Anima Christi – a thanksgiving for communion

Soul of Christ, sanctify me.
Body of Christ, save me.
Blood of Christ, fill me.
Water from the side of Christ, wash me.
Passion of Christ, strengthen me.
O good Jesus, hear me.
Within your wounds hide me.
Suffer me not to be separated from you.
From the malicious enemy defend me.
In the hour of my death call me.
And bid me come unto you.
That with your saints I may praise you.
For ever and ever.

After a sudden death

God of hope,
we come to you in shock and grief and confusion
        of heart.
Help us to find peace in the knowledge
        of your loving mercy to all your children,
and give us light to guide us out of our darkness
into the assurance of your love,
in Jesus Christ our Lord. **Amen.**

For those who mourn

Support us, O Lord,
all the day long of this troublous life,
until the shadows lengthen and the evening comes,
the busy world is hushed,
the fever of life is over
and our work is done.
Then, Lord, in your mercy grant us a safe lodging,
a holy rest, and peace at the last;
through Christ our Lord. **Amen.**

For the New Year

Eternal Lord God,
we give you thanks for bringing us
through the changes of time
to the beginning of another year.
Forgive us the wrong we have done
in the year that is past,
and help us to spend the rest of our days
to your honour and glory;
through Jesus Christ our Lord.

Serenity

God grant me the serenity to accept the things
        I cannot change,
courage to change the things I can,
and wisdom to know the difference.

Attributed to Reinhold Niebuhr (1892–1971)

A Muslim prayer from the Qur'an

This is the opening prayer of the Qur'an, the Muslim
scriptures, and is used regularly and as a blessing prayer
for or at the time of death.

In the Name of God, the Compassionate, the Merciful.
Praise be to God, Lord of the Worlds,
The Compassionate, the Merciful,
Master of the day of Judgement.
You we worship and of you we ask help.
Guide us upon the straight path;
The path of those whom you have blessed;
Not of those who have incurred your wrath
Nor of those who have gone astray.

Don't forget

O Lord! Thou knowest how busy I must be this day:
If I forget Thee do not thou forget me.

Prayer of Sir Jacob Astley (1579–1652)
before the battle of Edgehill in 1642

Teach us

Teach us, good Lord,
to serve thee as thou deservest;
to give and not to count the cost;
to fight and not to heed the wounds;
to toil and not to seek for rest;
to labour and not to ask for any reward
save that of knowing that we do thy will.

St Ignatius Loyola (1491–1556)

Prayer for animals

O God, enlarge within us a sense of fellowship with all living things, our brothers and sisters the animals, to whom you gave the earth as their home in common with us.

We remember with shame that in the past we have exercised the high dominion of humankind with ruthless cruelty, so that the voice of the earth, which should have gone up to you in song, has been a groan of travail.

May we realize that they live not for us alone but for themselves and for you, and that they love the sweetness of life.

St Basil (330–79)

St Teresa's Bookmark

Let nothing disturb thee,
Nothing affright thee;
All things are passing:
God never changeth.
Patient endurance
Attaineth to all things.
Who God possesseth
In nothing is wanting.
Alone God sufficeth.

St Teresa of Avila (1515–82)

From the Methodist Covenant Prayer

We are no longer our own, but yours.
Put us to what you will, rank us with whom you will;
put us to doing, put us to suffering;

let us be employed for you or laid aside for you,
exalted for you or brought low for you;
let us be full, let us be empty;
let us have all things, let us have nothing.
We freely and wholeheartedly yield all things
to your pleasure and disposal.
And now, glorious and blessed God,
Father, Son, and Holy Spirit,
you are ours and we are yours.
So be it.
and the covenant which we made on earth,
let it be ratified in heaven.

A prayer for Africa

God bless Africa;
Guard her children;
Guide her leaders
And give her peace, for Jesus Christ's sake. **Amen.**

Add your favourite prayers

_____

_____

_____

_____

_____

_____

_____

_____

Christian confidence

Daily bread

You will be familiar, as are all Christians, with the Lord's Prayer. We are to pray every day. The prayer asks, 'Give us this day our daily bread.' This means not only our food needs but also our spiritual and emotional needs. We get this especially from the regular reading of the Bible.

Jesus said, 'It is written, "One does not live by bread alone, but by every word that comes from the mouth of God."' (Matthew 4.4) Things that are written down often seem more important than things that are spoken. The spoken word is soon lost in the next sentence, while you can go back and read again what is written, so that you can work out its full meaning. But when God speaks, we all want to listen and to be able to reflect on what he is telling us. So we write his words down and record the stories about his people. Reading God's word again and again is like eating our daily bread, it keeps us going, fills us up and sets us up for the day. That is why Christians read the Bible.

Regular reading of the Bible will help you on your Christian pilgrimage. This chapter will show you how to get the most from your reading and encourage you to make your Bible your friend along the way.

What's in a name?

You will hear different names for the Bible. It is often called Holy Scripture. The Bible falls into two main parts, the Old Testament and the New Testament. The Old Testament comes from the Hebrew Scriptures, the New

Testament from Greek writings. There may also be a third part, called the Apocrypha, some or all of which is not included in the Bibles of different churches.

There are lots of different versions of the Bible. This means that different writers, translators or publishers produce their own version of the same text in order to do a particular job. So, a version might be written so as to be more accessible to children, or a version might be full of notes, useful to the more serious student. Different versions are often different translations of the early texts. You may already have found your favourite but this choice may change as your needs change. Some Bibles are very old translations with wonderful use of formal or poetic words. Others are presented with a more relaxed style to help with reading. Experiment with different translations and find the one that helps you to read more of the Bible. Perhaps your church uses one particular version and that may be the best one for you. Ask which version is usually read aloud at services in your church.

The version used throughout this book is the New Revised Standard Version. This is often recognized as the version which values traditional language while being accessible to the modern reader. This version has a high scholarly standard.

Other popular versions include:

- the Authorized Version: traditional and historic language from the time of King James I;
- the New International Version: a popular modern version with helpful headings that is easy to read and study;
- the Good News Bible: a popular modern version that can be suggested to younger readers. The version has helpful illustrations.

What's in it?

The Old Testament: the Scriptures of the Hebrew people that tell the story of God's relationship with his people. These are the books of the Old Testament:

Genesis	Ecclesiastes
Exodus	Song of Solomon
Leviticus	Isaiah
Numbers	Jeremiah
Deuteronomy	Lamentations
Joshua	Ezekiel
Judges	Daniel
Ruth	Hosea
1 Samuel	Joel
2 Samuel	Amos
1 Kings	Obadiah
2 Kings	Jonah
1 Chronicles	Micah
2 Chronicles	Nahum
Ezra	Habakkuk
Nehemiah	Zephaniah
Esther	Haggai
Job	Zechariah
Psalms	Malachi
Proverbs	

The New Testament: the writings about Jesus and the birth of the Church. These are the books of the New Testament:

Matthew	1 Timothy
Mark	2 Timothy
Luke	Titus
John	Philemon
Acts of the Apostles	Hebrews
Romans	James
1 Corinthians	1 Peter
2 Corinthians	2 Peter
Galatians	1 John
Ephesians	2 John
Philippians	3 John
Colossians	Jude
1 Thessalonians	Revelation
2 Thessalonians	

When you want to find a particular passage in the Bible, always turn to the contents page if you are uncertain where the book comes. This saves time and avoids you feeling silly when you can't find what you want. A useful tool is another book called a concordance that works a bit like an index to the whole Bible. If you look up a particular word, it will guide you to all the places that word appears, so you can find and choose the text you want.

You will most likely know by now how to look up a Bible reference, but it is worth making sure. You may be unfamiliar with the abbreviation used for a book of the Bible. There will be a list of these abbreviations at the front of your Bible.

The whole of the Bible is divided into books, chapters and verses. So various references might look like this:

- Jn 3.16 means the Gospel according to John, chapter 3, verse 16.

- Isa. 9.1, 6 means Isaiah, chapter 9, verse 1 and verse 6.
- Rev. 22.1–5 means Revelation, chapter 22, verses 1 to 5 inclusive.
- Acts 8.4, 11.19 means Acts, chapter 8, verse 4, and chapter 11, verse 19 (of the same book).
- v. 4a, v. 7b means the first part of verse 4, the second part of verse 7.
- ff. means 'following', that is, read on from here.

So where do I start?

Most people want to start at the beginning. There is the temptation to try and read the Bible like any other book, from cover to cover, particularly when you are filled with good intentions, but that's not the way to start. Other Christians (especially your clergy and lay leaders) will be able to help you with directed reading, perhaps by reading a little each day with some notes to aid understanding. Also, specially chosen readings will be read in church during the course of the year, telling the Bible accounts in a way that will help you grow each time you share in the story.

It is, though, a help to have an understanding of what the Bible says to us. It does this in different ways:

- with historical record;
- interpretation;
- story;
- myth;
- eyewitness accounts;
- teaching.

The various books of the Bible were written at different dates by different people for different purposes. Consequently it is important not to take individual passages out of context, and to discover as much information about the text. We should all be as informed as possible when we read Scripture. You can find out when a particular text was written and who it was aimed at. What sources was the author using? What was his/her special interest? When reading a passage, be sure to read what went before and what happens after, as this will give you an idea of the context. You can use a Bible commentary to help with this process of exploration. Attending Bible study groups can also help.

An overview of the Bible

There is so much of wonder in the Bible that it is almost impossible to provide a summary. However, the shape of the Bible story is important for us all.

The first book of the Bible is called Genesis, which means 'origin'. It covers the time from creation to the slavery of the Israelites in Egypt. Chapters 1—11 tell of the beginning of life and the start of human history with Adam and Eve. Then comes the history of the ancestors of the Israelite people (chapters 12—50) beginning with Abraham and Sarah. The story unfolds of God's creation being marred by human violence but God separates out a family line to which he promises an increase in numbers, a land of their own and a relationship with God that will change the world. This is not a scientific approach but a way of telling the story of our origins with meaning.

The Book of Exodus is the history of the Israelite people led by Moses from Egypt to the Promised Land. God gives the Ten Commandments (20.1–17) and the Law to his people and makes a covenant with them. The next three books, Leviticus, Numbers and Deuteronomy, continue the working out of the chosen people of God.

Then there are the historical books such as Joshua, Judges, 1 and 2 Samuel, 1 and 2 Kings, 1 and 2 Chronicles, Ezra and Nehemiah. These tell of Israel's past, its wars and rulers such as David and Solomon. Here you can find familiar stories such as the call of Samuel (1 Samuel 3), David and Goliath (1 Samuel 17.1–58) and Solomon's judgement (1 Kings 3).

The books of the Prophets tell of God's ongoing conversation with his people as they disobey him and as he warns them about the future. These books include the great prophets Isaiah, Jeremiah and Ezekiel and the lesser prophetic writings of Hosea, Joel, Amos, Obadiah, Jonah, Micah, Nahum, Habakkuk, Zephaniah, Haggai, Zechariah and Malachi.

The Psalms are a great testimony to the worship of God through the ages. These hymns or spiritual songs tell of almost every possible concern and condition to help us pray. Many Christians use the Psalms every day in their prayers. Perhaps the most famous Psalm is 23 which begins 'The Lord is my shepherd'.

The New Testament starts with the four Gospels, Matthew, Mark, Luke and John. These tell of Jesus' ministry on earth. Each book has its own special interest and records different stories that taken together give us the 'Good News' about Jesus. Christians should read a Gospel as part of their regular Bible study. The Gospels are meant to change the life of the reader. Sometimes the Gospel writers are called Evangelists.

The Acts of the Apostles comes next, written by the same author as the Gospel of Luke. This is the story of the early Church and of the first Christians. The Holy Spirit comes to empower the Church to spread the message that Jesus is risen from the dead. This message, taken by people like Peter and Paul, is to go to the whole world.

The way the early Church communicated, other than by word of mouth, was by letter. All of the remaining books of the New Testament are letters in one form or another. Some, like the Letters to the Corinthians, are to a specific community that is trying to find its way in the early days of church life. Others, like the Letters of Peter, are written to church leaders. All these are often called Epistles.

The last book of the Bible is called Revelation or the Apocalypse. This does a similar job to the Book of Daniel in the Old Testament. Revelation is a wonderful but often difficult book, crammed full of picture stories that stimulate the imagination. Many of the accounts contain special meanings and symbols that act almost like a code for understanding. Revelation culminates in a vision of heaven and with the wonderful words, 'Come, Lord Jesus!'

If you are going to read continuously it is always best to start with the Gospels and then perhaps follow this way into Scripture:

Read: one of the (Synoptic) Gospels, Matthew, Mark, Luke

Then: The Acts of the Apostles
            The Book of Isaiah
            The Gospel of John
            The Psalms
            The Book of Genesis
            The New Testament Letters

Passages of power

There are certain parts of the Bible that we should all know and be able to find. Now here are some famous passages that you will want to know, as they will enable God to use you to his glory.

The creation	Genesis 1 and 2
Noah and the flood	Genesis 6—9
The tower of Babel	Genesis 11
The call of Abram	Genesis 12
The command to sacrifice Isaac	Genesis 22
Isaac blesses Jacob	Genesis 27
Jacob's dream at Bethel	Genesis 28
Joseph, his brothers and Egypt	Genesis 37ff.
Moses and the people in slavery	Exodus 1ff.
The Passover	Exodus 12

Crossing the Red Sea	Exodus 14
Bread from heaven	Exodus 16
The Ten Commandments	Exodus 20,
	Deuteronomy 5
The fall of the walls of Jericho	Joshua 6
Samson and Delilah	Judges 14ff.
The call of Samuel	1 Samuel 3
Samuel anoints Saul	1 Samuel 10
David and Goliath	1 Samuel 17
God's covenant with David	2 Samuel 7
Solomon's judgement	1 Kings 3
The Queen of Sheba visits Solomon	1 Kings 10
Elijah ascends to heaven	2 Kings 2
The book of the law is found	2 Kings 22
'The people who walked in darkness'	Isaiah 9
'A shoot shall come out of Jesse'	Isaiah 11
'I have called you by name'	Isaiah 43
The Suffering Servant	Isaiah 54
'Arise, shine; for your light has come'	Isaiah 60
'The spirit of the Lord is upon me'	Isaiah 61
'Before I formed you in the womb	
I knew you'	Jeremiah 1
The psalm of personal distress	Lamentations 3
The valley of dry bones	Ezekiel 37
Water flowing from the temple	Ezekiel 47
Daniel in the lions' den	Daniel 6
Jonah and the whale	Jonah 1—4
'O Bethlehem of Ephrathah'	Micah 5
The coming messenger	Malachi 3

(Where an account appears in more than one of the Gospels it is given the reference from Matthew but * indicates that it can also be found in one or more of the other Gospels.)

The birth of Jesus	Matthew 1ff.*
John the Baptist	Matthew 3*
The temptation in the wilderness	Matthew 4*
The call of the disciples	Matthew 4*
The Sermon on the Mount	Matthew 5*
The Lord's Prayer	Matthew 6*
The Centurion's servant	Matthew 8*
The stilling of the storm	Matthew 8*
The healing of the paralysed man	Matthew 9*
The names of the disciples	Matthew 10*
Teaching about the Sabbath	Matthew 12*
Teaching in parables	Matthew 13*
Feeding the five thousand	Matthew 14*
Jesus walks on water	Matthew 14*
Feeding the four thousand	Matthew 15*
The Transfiguration	Matthew 17*
Teaching about children	Matthew 18* 19*
Teaching on marriage	Matthew 19*
A rich person entering heaven	Matthew 19*
Labourers in the vineyard	Matthew 20
Palm Sunday	Matthew 21*
Cleansing the Temple	Matthew 21*
The marriage feast	Matthew 22*

Jesus and the Samaritans	John 4
Healing of a lame man on the Sabbath	John 5
Jesus, the bread of life	John 6
Jesus, the water of life	John 7
Jesus, the light of the world	John 9
Jesus, the good shepherd	John 10
The raising of Lazarus	John 11
The anointing at Bethany	John 12
Jesus washes the feet of his disciples	John 13
'I am the way, and the truth, and the life'	John 14
Jesus, the true vine	John 15
The prayer of Jesus	John 17
Doubting Thomas	John 20
The commissioning of Peter	John 21
The ascension of Jesus	Acts 1
The day of Pentecost	Acts 2
The death of Stephen	Acts 7
The conversion of Saul	Acts 9
Being justified by faith	Romans 5
Life in the Spirit	Romans 8
The Lord's Supper	1 Corinthians 11
Spiritual gifts	1 Corinthians 12
Love	1 Corinthians 13
The significance for us of the resurrection	1 Corinthians 15
The humility of Christ	Philippians 2
The cloud of witnesses	Hebrews 12
The vision of God	Revelation 5ff.
The new heaven and the new earth	Revelation 21

Regular reading

It will take a lifetime to study the Bible. Begin by reading just a little every day, perhaps by starting off with the passages above, reading one a day. Remember, a Bible is to be used, not kept as an ornament. God will find his way to you through the words on paper and you will soon find that he speaks to you through your reading. Never give up – if you fail, just start again and ask God to help you. With the Bible as your daily bread, you will never go hungry.

I believe

Your confirmation classes will have prepared you well for the growth of your faith, but it is useful to have a reminder of our basic articles of belief.

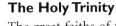

The Holy Trinity

The great faiths of the world, Christianity, Judaism and Islam, all believe in one God (monotheism) and we all share common roots.

Christians are able to express their faith in terms of the Trinity because of the unique revelation through Jesus Christ and the gift of the Holy Spirit described in Acts chapter 2.

One classic explanation of this understanding of God is used in many confirmation classes. Water, ice and steam are all forms of the same substance but different forms. God is so wonderful that he has shown himself to us in three different but remarkable ways. The Trinity is an expression of relationship and thereby of love. 'God is love and those who abide in love abide in God, and God abides in them' (1 John 4.16).

In the Nicene Creed we state our belief that the Almighty God, the creator of heaven and earth, who from all eternity is the Father of Jesus, is also our Father. This belief stems from the teaching of Jesus in the New Testament that the creator is not some distant essence in the cosmos but a loving Father from whom his co-equal Son comes forth from all eternity. This is a God of relationship, of powerful love that gives force to a person in its own right, the Holy Spirit. Jesus said, 'I will ask the Father, and he will give you another Advocate, to be with you for ever' (John 14.16).

Belief in the Trinity is common to all the historic churches and is part of that which binds us together, despite our petty divisions. When you were baptized the words used for you, and for all Christians were these:

N, I baptize you
in the name of the Father,
and of the Son,
and of the Holy Spirit. **Amen.**

The Collect for Trinity Sunday summarizes this belief:

Almighty and everlasting God,
you have given us your servants grace,
by the confession of a true faith,
to acknowledge the glory of the eternal Trinity
and in the power of the divine majesty to worship
    the Unity:
keep us steadfast in this faith,
that we may evermore be defended from all adversities;
through Jesus Christ your Son our Lord,
who is alive and reigns with you,
in the unity of the Holy Spirit,
one God, now and for ever.

If we believe God to be in relationship with humankind, this is most obvious in Jesus Christ his Son, our Lord. Jesus was a real, historical person, born into our world, who shared our life experiences. We believe that Jesus became truly human and that in his life and death God is present for all. We speak

of Jesus as our Saviour because by his death and resurrection
he has promised salvation to all who follow him.

The Holy Spirit is God himself, coming into our hearts and
active among us in liberating words and deeds. We celebrate
the Holy Spirit most especially on the feast of Pentecost.

At a baptism, the church, together with the candidates
and/or their sponsors make this profession of faith. We are
asked if we believe and trust, our hearts being open to God
yet trusting that we will come to believe more deeply.

Do you believe and trust in God the Father?
**I believe in God, the Father almighty,
creator of heaven and earth.**

Do you believe and trust in his Son Jesus Christ?
**I believe in Jesus Christ, his only Son, our Lord,
who was conceived by the Holy Spirit,
born of the Virgin Mary,
suffered under Pontius Pilate,
was crucified, died, and was buried;
he descended to the dead.
On the third day he rose again;
he ascended into heaven,
he is seated at the right hand of the Father,
and he will come to judge the living and the dead.**

Do you believe and trust in the Holy Spirit?
**I believe in the Holy Spirit,
the holy catholic Church,
the communion of saints,
the forgiveness of sins,
the resurrection of the body,
and the life everlasting. Amen.**

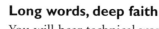

Long words, deep faith

You will hear technical words used about our faith. Here is a useful summary of some of the main phrases.

Incarnation

Jesus, being born into human existence, sharing our life, God among us. This means that God is involved in creation, active, participating in our world.

Resurrection

On the third day after his death, Jesus rose again and promised the same to those who believe. This will be new life in Christ beyond the grave.

Redemption

To be delivered from sin and restored to full relationship and communion with God.

Atonement

At-one-ment, our reconciliation with God through the sacrificial death of Christ.

Parousia

The second coming of Jesus as judge of the world.

Theology

Talking and thinking about matters to do with God.

I belong to the Church

You are a confirmed member of the Church of England, which is part of the Anglican Communion, which is part of the one, holy, catholic and apostolic Church. You are therefore an Anglican.

This means that you belong to a much wider community than just your own. Everybody in England lives in a *parish*, which in turn is part of a *deanery*, that is part of an *archdeaconry*, that is part of a *diocese*, that is in a *province*, that is in the *Church of England*, that is in the *Anglican Communion*, that is part of the worldwide *Church*. You can include your own details here:

My parish is called: _____

My deanery is called: _____

My archdeaconry is called: _____

My diocese is called: _____

My province is called: _____

which is part of the Church of England in the Anglican Communion which is part of the whole Church of God in Christ Jesus.

When you were baptized you joined the whole Church, not just the Church of England. All baptized Christians belong to the Church of Christ, hence the name Christian. However, owing to divisions over the centuries, the Church has different denominations with different understandings and affiliations. However, the historic churches share a common baptism and a common belief in the Trinity.

This means that when we speak about 'the Church', we may be speaking about all Christians together or our own Anglican part of it or even our local Christian community or even a building!

A pocket history

The Church began with Jesus himself, his call of the disciples and their struggle to spread the Good News. On the Day of Pentecost the disciples and others were gathered together in one place, and the Holy Spirit rested upon them, giving them the power to build new communities. The apostles travelled through the known world leaving behind, as the fruit of their ministry and preaching, small churches that grew despite their persecution by those around them.

In the fourth century the Emperor Constantine adopted Christianity and the Church grew beyond all expectation. Over the centuries the Church became a powerful force in people's lives and in affairs of state. In time, Christianity split into two main parts, the Western Church based in Rome and the Eastern Orthodox Church based in Constantinople.

Between the fourteenth and seventeenth centuries the Reformation took place as the Western Church tore itself apart because of fundamental disagreements. The greatest division was between Catholics and Protestants (those who protest). The Reformation was clouded not only by theological differences but also by political power struggles. This was true particularly in England. There were strong movements towards enabling the people to participate in their faith more fully – for example by having access to the Bible translated into English, and having a worship book that could be used by ordinary worshippers – and there was a general need for freedom that was seeking expression. However, things came to a head in the political world of the day.

King Henry VIII needed to end his childless marriage to Catherine of Aragon in order to provide an heir. The Pope refused to allow this and so Henry broke with Rome. The English monarch became Supreme Governor of the Church of England which introduced its own theological and liturgical reforms. However, the apostolic succession of bishops remained intact. The Church of England became the established church of our land.

Further divisions came and other churches grew, such as the Methodist Church or the Baptist Church or the United Reformed Church.

These days the churches work together in a spirit of partnership so that our historical differences do not hold us back from a common witness.

Working together

The common commitment of the churches in England is not meaningless. Great efforts are made, especially locally, to work in harmony. This means honouring our differences as well as celebrating our similarities. As Anglicans, our church is part of Churches Together in England. Ask your church community about events organized by your local grouping.

The churches also strive for unity on the international front in the hope that, as Jesus prayed, 'we may all be one'.

Around the world there are sister Anglican churches who belong to the Anglican Communion or family of churches. These all relate to the Archbishop of Canterbury. Here is a statement that summarizes our understanding as a church, called the Preface to the Declaration of Assent.

> The Church of England is part of the one, holy, catholic, and apostolic Church, worshipping the one true God, Father, Son, and Holy Spirit. It professes the faith uniquely revealed in the holy Scriptures and set forth in the catholic creeds, which faith the Church is called upon to proclaim afresh in each generation. Led by the Holy Spirit, it has borne witness to Christian truth in its historic formularies, the Thirty-Nine Articles of Religion, the Book of Common Prayer, and the ordering of Bishops, Priests, and Deacons.

People and places

Every human organization has its own life and the Church of England is no exception. Here are some simple descriptions to help you understand the complex life of our busy church.

Church government

We have a dual system. The House of Bishops consists of our spiritual leaders and they work through a partnership with an elected group called the General Synod. This is similar to an elected parliament, meeting to discuss matters of importance, policy and mission.

The Archbishop of Canterbury

The Archbishop is the Primate of all England and Metropolitan, which means he is the leader of the Church of England and the Anglican Communion. He lives and works at Lambeth Palace in London although he is also responsible for the Diocese of Canterbury. An archbishop is responsible for a province, which is a grouping of dioceses.

The Province of Canterbury includes the following dioceses: Bath and Wells, Birmingham, Bristol, Canterbury, Chelmsford, Chichester, Coventry, Derby, Ely, Europe, Exeter, Gloucester, Guildford, Hereford, Leicester, Lichfield, Lincoln, London, Norwich, Oxford, Peterborough, Portsmouth, Rochester, St Albans, St Edmundsbury and Ipswich, Salisbury, Southwark, Truro, Winchester, Worcester.

The Archbishop of York has in his Province:
Blackburn, Bradford, Carlisle, Chester, Durham, Liverpool, Manchester, Newcastle, Ripon and Leeds, Sheffield, Sodor and Man, Southwell, Wakefield, York.

A bishop

A bishop is the spiritual leader of a diocese, which is a historic geographical area as above.

My diocese is: _____

_____

My Bishop is: _____

The bishop who confirmed me was: _____

_____

There are also area or suffragan bishops who assist diocesan bishops. All bishops bear the title 'The Right Reverend' in front of their name. A bishop has special clothing for his role, which may include a purple cassock, a rochet and chimere, a cope, mitre, episcopal ring and pastoral staff (but not all at the same time!).

A dean

This person is responsible for the running of a cathedral. He or she has the title 'The Very Reverend' in front of their name. Every diocese has a cathedral.

An archdeacon

This person is responsible for an archdeaconry that is an area within a diocese. An archdeacon is a person who is part of the bishop's staff, helping with the pastoral administration of a diocese. He or she has the title 'The Venerable' in front of their name.

A canon

There are two main types of canon, clergy whose job it is to work in a cathedral, helping the dean, and other senior clergy who have an additional responsibility in a diocese or who have given outstanding service.

A rural (or area) dean

Their role is to work with other local clergy and lay people to care for neighbouring churches, in a small area of a number of parishes.

An incumbent, or rector, or vicar or priest in charge

All these are various names for the priest responsible for a parish. Every part of the country is in a parish.

An assistant curate

This person is usually in training and may be for a time a deacon. Later they may be ordained priest. There are several other titles for assistant clergy, especially those who offer their ministry without financial charge to the church. Why not find out what the titles and responsibilities of your parish clergy are?

Chaplain

There are many types of clergy whose task is to work for a specific organization or to care for a group. Examples might be hospital chaplains, prison chaplains and forces chaplains.

So looking at the above, you will live in a parish, which is in a deanery, which is in an archdeaconry, which is in a diocese, which is in a province, which is part of the Church of England, which is part of the Anglican Communion, which is part of the worldwide Christian Church.

Visiting a church

Church buildings are very varied. Two thousand years of church building mean that we have small rooms, ancient chapels, majestic churches and powerful cathedrals all dedicated to the glory of God.

It may be helpful to look at the main parts of a church, and their technical names, whatever the architectural style of the church you belong to.

East, west, north and south

If this seems a strange order for the points of the compass this

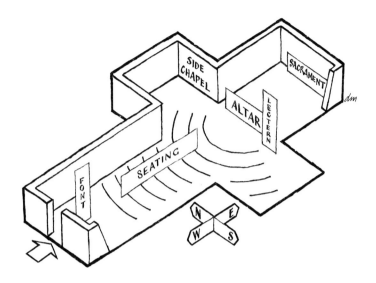

is because most churches are built so that the way people face is east, facing the Holy Land, the way people leave is west, out into the world. I well remember a true story from my last church. During a children's talk, when we were all learning about the meaning of our church building, I took the children to the east end and, having explained earlier about Jerusalem, I pointed east and asked the question, 'And if you keep going this way where do you finally come to?' The confident reply came back from a very young voice, 'Tesco's!' We should never take our buildings or our children for granted.

The place of Baptism

Often the first piece of furniture that you will come across as you enter a church (apart from the bookstall!) is a font. This is traditionally placed near the door in order to be the entry turnstile, be baptized and come on in. The font should be filled with water and regularly used. Nearby there may well be a large candle, also called the Paschal Candle, which is used to light the candles used in Holy Baptism and especially in Eastertide.

The place of the people

However your church is arranged, there will be a place for the people to sit. This is often called the nave. Historically, the nave was the place of meeting for a community as well as the place of gathering for worship. We should remember that God has given us our buildings for use rather than for museums. Naves are for sitting in, standing in, meeting in and for moving around.

The place of the word

There is often a lectern and a pulpit for the proclamation of the Liturgy of the Word. Sometimes the lectern is in the shape of an eagle, carrying the word of God to the people, and the pulpit recalls Jesus standing on the boat on the Sea of Galilee so that the people could hear him.

The place of other ministers and of music

Sometimes called the chancel or the choir, this is often the place that other helpers gather and where the choir may sit. The Church is blessed with many wonderful musicians and singers who offer to God praise in many amazing ways.

The place of the sacrament

Sometimes called the sanctuary, this is the place where the

Eucharistic Prayer is offered. The priest, sometimes helped by servers, stands here on behalf of the whole people of God to offer the sacrifice of Jesus himself. This may be the most highly decorated part of the church.

The place of prayer

A church is really a place of prayer, set aside for your use and for God's glory. There may be special side chapels or places for daily prayer or for candle lighting or community activities. All these things are important. But more than anything else, we must always remember that the Church is not the building, or the structure, or the important person but the people of God.

Why not take time to learn about your own church building to see what it is saying to you and to God?

Christian action

'Stand by for action'

This will date me but you may just remember that at the beginning of the children's television programme *Stingray*, the announcement with enormous confidence is 'Stand by for action!' It may not always seem like it but that is exactly how we should feel as Christians about sharing our faith.

As Christians we are called to worship and to know God with confidence. We are also called to proclaim the Good News of Jesus Christ in the world. We are called to put our faith into action. This means that we have to be involved in everyday life as Christians, not retreating from the world as if we have a treasure that cannot be shared. Jesus often found moments to withdraw from society in order to pray and to 'recharge his batteries' but in the main he spent his ministry in the full glare of publicity. Jesus was God born into our world, to engage with it, to bring people back into relationship with our creator. Jesus came to make a difference.

We all share in this ministry today. We all have a part to play. You are a disciple, an evangelist, and an apostle. Every Christian is called to witness to Jesus in their own place and to lead others to know him. There are many different ways in which this takes place.

Mission

To continue the *Stingray* theme, the next announcement is 'Anything can happen in the next half hour!' When we go out into the world, we should believe that God can work miracles through us. We may not often be able to astound those around us but we should believe that through our actions God will work and his will is done. To be engaged with the world around us, to be focused on our role in society, to be active in service is to 'do' mission. The mission of the Church is to proclaim Christ. Jesus' great commission to his disciples at the very end of his time on earth tells us our task.

> Now the eleven disciples went to Galilee, to the mountain to which Jesus had directed them. When they saw him, they worshipped him; but some doubted. And Jesus came and said to them, 'All authority in heaven and on earth has been given to me. Go therefore and make disciples of all nations, baptizing them in the name of the Father and of the Son and of the Holy Spirit, and teaching them to obey everything that I have commanded you. And remember, I am with you always, to the end of the age.'
>
> Matthew 28.16–20

If we are determined to do this, anything can happen, although it may just take longer than half an hour!

Mission comes in many different forms. Sometimes it may be a concerted programme of contact and promotion of Christian events organized to attract new people who may not have heard about Jesus before or who may have ignored his message. Sometimes it may be as simple as the Church doing a funeral really well so that people see and feel the love of Christ in a tangible way. Sometimes it may be a powerful sermon that stirs the heart into response. By far and away the best and most productive form of mission is undertaken by every individual Christian or Christians working together to show Christ by their words and actions. The old phrase 'practising what you preach' still rings true today. You may be very new to the Church or returning after many years, but you have a part to play in the mission of Jesus Christ.

Evangelism

If mission is doing, evangelism is telling. We are all called to be evangelists. The Gospel writers, Matthew, Mark, Luke and John, are called evangelists because they told the story of Jesus. Likewise, but in our own way, we are called to tell others about Christ. Some do this on the street corner, hoping indifferent people will grasp the moment, others tell the story more subtly and with more dignity in personal conversations or testimonies. A testimony is simply your story of relationship with Jesus, told in your own words. Sometimes we are called to do this in public, to give others hope, and sometimes we are called to do this in quiet moments with someone who is searching for their way forward. All Christians are called to mission and evangelism. Ask your church about its mission. Are they standing by for action? What are you going to do for Jesus in the next half hour?

Being a Christian today

You will remember the wonderful feeling when you were confirmed. You will also remember how anxious and uncertain you may have been when you first took the plunge to come forward and ask about the growing faith inside you. Being a Christian in the twenty-first century is not easy. It's not trendy, it's not always popular, even among those close to us. But it is beyond comparison as a way of life and as a way to God.

Life and freedom

Christianity is too often portrayed as a faith full of dos and don'ts, with more don'ts than dos. This is not true. We have a God who has made us to have the most from life possible. God has made us free and able to choose, which is the wonder of creation. But God knows that to get the most out of life, we must put a great deal in also and that 'having it all' does not make us happy.

This is true of money, property, relationships and status. We have to take responsibility for our actions and live in community. God wants us to live life to the full and gives us a way of life through the Bible and the teaching of the Christian community. Have faith in God's way: it leads to wholeness, healing, hope and life everlasting.

Caring for each other

God has placed us in a wonderful environment and we share with him in caring for it. We all can play our part in our stewardship of the world and its resources. Christians have a special calling to this responsibility.

We also have a calling to each other, in caring for those in need and for the common life of the Church.

Another aspect of our common life is the sharing of our resources with each other and with the Church, our time, our talents or our money. Every organization needs funding to exist, especially when we consider our public ministry, our mission and our wonderful buildings built to the glory of God. Ask someone in your church about your financial giving.

A rule of life

If we are going to make sense of our lives we need to prepare for our growing commitment. It is always best to plan for a journey and to have staging posts along the way. One way of doing this is to prepare a rule of life. This is a plan of your daily or weekly life as a Christian. You may like to write down the following:

- what time of day you are going to set aside for *prayer*;
- how you are going to read the *Bible* regularly;
- how often you are going to receive *Holy Communion*;
- what *financial giving* you will choose as your *commitment*;
- whom you are going to help as a form of *service*;
- what study or *course* you are going to engage in;
- when you are going to *review* your rule of life.

No such plan should be a wish list that is unachievable or too holy. Your parish priest or another spiritual director will be able to help you to prepare and review such a plan. This is a really mature way of ordering your spiritual life so that you have principles to work by.

Who, me?

All the way through this book I have spoken of 'calling'.

By being baptized, all Christians have a ministry and a calling or vocation. God has a plan for each one of us as to what he wants us to do in life.

For some it will be a career of service to others, for some it will be a vocation to family life, for some it will be to teach, for some it may be to pray and for some it may be to public ministry in the Church. Discerning your vocation as a Christian is a major aspect of confirmed status.

As you grow into Christian life, you will discover more about what God has in mind. Then, as you test this calling you may find that this can change the course of your life. People often speak about vocation in its narrowest sense as a vocation to the ordained ministry. But vocation influences every walk of life. But it may just be that you feel it right at some point in the future to test a vocation to ordination or another form of public ministry and the Church is standing ready to help you discern your call. Simply speak to someone you recognize in authority in your church. Beware – 'anything can happen in the next half hour.'

Conclusion

This book is meant to help you on your developing journey of faith. It is about continuing your confirmation commitment. There may be days when you will feel far from God or periods when you have lapsed in your participation in the Christian life, but never fear. God is with us and is always there for you – yes, you!

At your confirmation, the bishop may well have used these words to help you on your way. With the help of God, you will confirm the faith in you.

Those who are baptized are called to worship and serve God.

Will you continue in the apostles' teaching and fellowship,
   in the breaking of bread, and in the prayers?
With the help of God, I will.

Will you persevere in resisting evil,
   and, whenever you fall into sin, repent and return to
   the Lord?
With the help of God, I will.

Will you proclaim by word and example
   the good news of God in Christ?
With the help of God, I will.

Will you seek and serve Christ in all people,
  loving your neighbour as yourself?
With the help of God, I will.

Will you acknowledge Christ's authority over human
  society,
by prayer for the world and its leaders,
by defending the weak, and by seeking peace and justice?
With the help of God, I will.

May Christ dwell in your hearts through faith,
that you may be rooted and grounded in love
and bring forth the fruit of the Spirit. **Amen.**

Glossary

Here is a short list of words and their brief meanings to help you in your understanding of the Church.

Abba	the Aramaic word for 'Father' used by Jesus
Advent	'Coming', the season running up to Christmas
Agnus Dei	Latin for 'Lamb of God', a song used after the breaking of the bread at the Eucharist
alb	long, white garment worn by servers and clergy at the Eucharist
Amen	So be it!
Annunciation	25 March, the 'announcement' of the birth of Jesus to Mary by the Archangel Gabriel
apostle	a follower of Jesus, one of the twelve disciples, or someone like St Paul
Ascension	Christ's return to heaven, celebrated ten days before Pentecost
Ash Wednesday	the first day of Lent
banns (of marriage)	the legal notification of a forthcoming marriage
BCP	1662 Book of Common Prayer

Beatitudes	the beginning of the Sermon on the Mount describing the Christian life (Matthew 5.3–11)
canticle	a scriptural song used in worship
cassock	long, often black garment worn by clergy as their main dress for services
chalice	cup used at communion
chasuble	the outermost garment worn by priests at the Eucharist, usually in the liturgical colour of the day
chrism	the oil blessed by the bishop for use at Baptism, Confirmation and Ordinations
churchwardens	the elected lay leaders of Church of England churches
ciborium	chalice shaped vessel, with a lid, used at communion for the eucharistic bread
Collect	the short prayer that is related to the day at the Eucharist
concordance	a reference book to help find individual passages of Scripture
cope	a flowing cape used by clergy in processions
creed	statement of faith
deacon	an ordained person with particular responsibility for service to those in need, and for proclaiming the Gospel in acts of worship

dean	usually the priest responsible for a cathedral
doxology	ending of a prayer such as 'Glory to the Father and to the Son and to the Holy Spirit; as it was in the beginning is now and shall be for ever. Amen.'
ecumenical action	different denominations of Christian churches working together
Epiphany	from the Greek for 'manifestation' – celebrates the 'showing' of Jesus to the world, at the visit of the magi
Eucharist	the Greek word meaning 'thanksgiving' referring to the whole service of Holy Communion
font	holds the water for Holy Baptism
Gentiles	the biblical term to denote non-Jews
Holy Week	the week preceding Easter, recalling the last days of Jesus in Jerusalem
icons	devotional pictures and paintings mostly from the Eastern Orthodox churches, used for prayer
intercession	prayer on behalf of others and general needs
Jesus Christ	Jesus – the Greek form of the Hebrew name Joshua; Christ – the Greek for Messiah
Kyrie eleison	Greek for 'Lord, have mercy', a set of penitential

	sentences said or sung at the beginning of the Eucharist
Lambeth Palace	home of the Archbishop of Canterbury
lectern	furniture used in church from which the readings often take place
lectionary	a system of specially chosen readings to be read in worship
Lent	the forty days of preparation for Easter
litany	a set of short prayers, often in a long list, with responses
liturgy	meaning 'the work of the people', or the worship of the people of God
magi	Latin form of the Greek word for 'wise men' (Matthew 2.1–12)
matins	morning prayer from the BCP (Book of Common Prayer), often sung
Maundy Thursday	the commemoration of the Last Supper
mitre	the liturgical headwear of a bishop
Nicene Creed	the fourth-century summary of Christian faith used regularly at the Sunday Eucharist
office	one of the daily times of prayer, usually for morning or evening

Padre	a popular title for chaplains in the armed forces
parables	short stories told by Jesus comparing everyday life with spiritual truth
Paschal	concerning Easter
passion	Jesus' suffering and death
paten	the plate used for the bread at the Eucharist
president	the minister leading a service
pulpit	an elevated place from which a minister preaches a sermon
quire	the old spelling of choir
rector	the historic title of a priest who is responsible for more than one parish
repentance	being sorry for one's sins
retreat	a period of days spent away in silence or reflection
Reverend	the formal title of ordained men and women
sacrament	an outward and visible sign of an inward and spiritual gift
Sanctus	the Latin for 'holy', referring to the song 'Holy, holy, holy Lord' in the Eucharist
sidespersons	lay people who help with stewarding at services

synod	a meeting to make decisions in church government
Taizé	the ecumenical religious community in France known for its worship and music, and visited by thousands of young people
unction	anointing with holy oil and prayer for the sick to bring inner peace and healing
vestry	the room in church used for the preparations before services
vicar	the usual title for a parish priest
Whit Sunday	the old title for the Day of Pentecost

Directory

Here are some useful contact points that you might find helpful in the future.

The Church of England

Church House, Great Smith Street, London SW1P 3NZ
020 7898 1000

www.cofe.anglican.org
Follow links to all the Church's websites and much more.

Common Worship
Church House Publishing, Church House, Great Smith Street, London SW1P 3NZ

www.cofe.anglican.org/commonworship

Growing in faith

www.alphacourse.org.uk
Looking for answers? The Alpha course is an opportunity for anyone to explore the Christian faith in a relaxed, non-threatening manner over ten, thought-provoking weekly sessions.

Emmaus, the Way of Faith
A course designed to welcome people into Christian faith and the life of the Church. Emmaus enables the Church to build relationships with those outside the Church, accompany enquirers on their journey of faith and bring new Christians to maturity.
Published by The National Society/Church House Publishing.

Other useful addresses

www.learningchurch.org.uk
Adult learning resources run by Anglican national advisers.

www.spck.org.uk
The leading Christian booksellers and publishers.

www.scriptureunion.org.uk
Resources for everything to do with Bible reading and teaching.

www.churcharmy.org.uk
Sharing faith in Jesus Christ through words and action.

www.rscm.com
The Royal School of Church Music

www.brf.org.uk
The Bible Reading Fellowship, daily Bible reading notes.

www.churches-together.org.uk
The website of Churches Together in England

In emergency

The Samaritans   0845 790 9090
'Whatever you're going through, we'll go through it with you.'

Childline
(Children requiring counselling)
Freepost 111, London N1   Linkline 0800 1111

Sources and acknowledgements

The author and publisher gratefully acknowledge permission to reproduce copyright material. Every effort has been made to trace and acknowledge copyright holders. The publisher apologizes for any omissions and, if notified, will ensure that full acknowledgements are made in a subsequent edition of this book.

Buckley, Michael, 'For the confirmed', *The Treasure of the Holy Spirit*, p. 58, Hodder & Stoughton 1984.

Common Worship: Services and Prayers for the Church of England, Church House Publishing 2000. Extracts are reproduced by permission of Church House Publishing.

Cottrell, Stephen, 'A Girl Guide Grace' and 'May Our Lord Jesus Christ' (both on p. 13), *Praying through Life*, National Society/ Church House Publishing 1998. Extracts from *Praying Through Life* (National Society/Church House Publishing, 1998) are copyright © Stephen Cottrell 1998 and are reproduced by permission of the publishers.

Dudley-Smith, Timothy, 'Evening Prayer (Tell Out, My Soul)' is reproduced with the author's permission.

Kumar, Satish, 'Lead us from death to life' is reproduced with the author's permission.

Niebuhr, Reinhold, 'Serenity' in Deborah Cassidi (ed.), *Favourite Prayers*, Cassell 1998.

Pocket Ritual, Mayhew-McCrimmon 1977.

Oliver, Stephen, 'Blessed are you, Lord God', *Pastoral Prayers*, Mowbray 1996.

Saward, Michael, 'O Lord, enable us this day' is reproduced with the author's permission.

Society of Saint Francis, 'Evening Prayer', *The Daily Office*, p. 112, Society of Saint Francis 1981, 1986. Reproduced by permission of the Society of Saint Francis.

The author and publisher would also like to thank Donald Mullis for permission to reproduce his illustrations throughout this book.